EURIPIDES · IV

Rhesus
The Suppliant Women
Orestes
Iphigenia in Aulis

THE COMPLETE GREEK TRAGEDIES

Edited by David Grene and Richmond Lattimore

EURIPIDES · IV

RHESUS
Translated by Richmond Lattimore

THE SUPPLIANT WOMEN
Translated by Frank Jones

ORESTES
Translated by William Arrowsmith

IPHIGENIA IN AULIS
Translated by Charles R. Walker

THE UNIVERSITY OF CHICAGO PRESS
CHICAGO & LONDON

THE UNIVERSITY OF CHICAGO PRESS, CHICAGO 60637
The University of Chicago Press, Ltd., London

© 1958 by The University of Chicago
All rights reserved. Published 1958
Printed in the United States of America

82 81 80 79 78   11 10 9 8 7

International Standard Book Number: 0–226–30783–2
Library of Congress Catalog Card Number: 55–5787

TABLE OF CONTENTS

RHESUS

Translated by Richmond Lattimore

INTRODUCTION TO *RHESUS*

The ancient Argument, or Introduction, to *Rhesus* contains the following statement: "Some have suspected that this play is spurious, that is, not by Euripides. For it shows a character which is more like Sophocles. Nevertheless, it is recorded in the play-lists as a genuine play of Euripides; and the overelaborateness [? Greek *polypragmosyne*] with which elevation is striven for is in the manner of Euripides." Who these "some" were we do not know, but it seems plain that their suspicions were based on internal, not external, evidence. The play was officially credited to Euripides. Further, from the notes (*scholia*) on the text, line 529, we have the following: "Crates says that Euripides was ignorant of astronomy in this passage because he was still young when he presented *Rhesus*."

Thus we may say that, while *Rhesus* was firmly attested as a play by Euripides, there was a feeling that there was something peculiar about it, that it did not read, feel, sound like Euripides. Modern critics have generally shared the uneasiness which the writer of our Argument felt, though they have not shared, or even understood, his notion that it is "more like Sophocles." While in this brief unscientific introduction I can offer no full treatment,[1] the following characteristics may be noted.

1. The action is taken direct from the Tenth Book of the *Iliad*. Its chief events, the sortie of Dolon, the countermission of Odysseus and Diomedes, who kill Dolon, and the death of Rhesus, are all in Homer, though there are changes in emphasis, particularly in the importance of the part played by Athene, the importance of Rhesus for the Trojan cause, and the introduction of the Muse as Rhesus' mother. This is the only extant tragedy which takes its material straight out of the *Iliad*.[2] The regular practice of the tragic poets

---

[1] Those who are curious about the "Rhesus question" are referred to C. B. Sneller, *De Rheso Tragoedia* (Amsterdam: H. J. Paris, 1949). This is full and thorough. There is an excellent briefer discussion in G. M. A. Grube, *The Drama of Euripides* (London: Methuen & Co., 1941), pp. 439–47.

[2] The fragments of tragedy offer only one other certain case, the trilogy by Aeschylus which contained *The Myrmidons*, *The Nereids*, and *The Ransoming of Hector*. It is

when they dealt with the heroes and stories of the Trojan War was to choose episodes which fell outside the scope of the *Iliad*, before its opening or, more frequently, after its close.

2. This is the only extant tragedy whose action all takes place at night. But this is dictated by the facts of the situation in Homer.

3. Fate and divine mechanics are used more baldly than elsewhere in tragedy.

"If Rhesus survives this day or night [but he will not] all will be well." This is a minor motive in Sophocles' *Ajax* and serves better as such than as a major motive, which it is here.

"If Rhesus fights tomorrow, Achilles, Ajax, and all the rest of the Greeks cannot stop him." Why on earth should we believe this? He might, of course, be played in a costume, with built-up boots, that makes him tower, giant-like, over Hector himself. But belief in Rhesus is plainly enforced because a god guarantees him (Athene, ll. 600–605). Athene also tells Odysseus whom to kill, whom not to kill, because it is or is not authorized or "fated" (ll. 633–36).

"If a man is too confident, even if that confidence is justified, or if others speak too well of him, he is doomed to destruction" (see ll. 342–87, 447–53). The tragic poets may sometimes say that men are puppets in the hands of the gods, but they do not elsewhere make them so in action. This machinery is bare.

4. The iambics of *Rhesus* show resolution (three syllables for two) in 8.6 per cent of the lines, on my count.[3] It is well known that in the period of his extant plays Euripides indulged more and more freely in resolution as time went on. His earliest dated play, *Alcestis* (438 B.C.), shows resolution of 6.5 per cent. His latest, the posthumous *Bacchae* and *Iphigenia in Aulis*, have 37.5 per cent and 48 per cent respectively. The rate of increase is by no means constant, but we may

---

striking that here Aeschylus also departed from the usual convention in using the theme of homosexual love, which I have not found elsewhere in tragedy. If he repeated neither experiment, perhaps that means that this trilogy was not well received.

[3] Statistical counts will vary because the scholar has some latitude in deciding whether certain feet, apparently of three syllables, might actually be run together and read as two. I also think it fairer to count proper names. Some do not. One can make mistakes, too. But the variations will not be significant.

say flatly that *Rhesus* cannot be a play written by Euripides after 415 and that it is probably far earlier. There is, however, one complication. *Rhesus* has trochees; it should not. All but one of the latest plays, beginning with *The Trojan Women* (415; iambic resolution 22.5 per cent), contain trochees. The only earlier play which has them is *Heracles*, which, on metrical and material grounds, can probably be put about 422–420 B.C. Its resolution rate is 19 per cent. No extant play with a resolution rate below that of *Heracles* has trochees, except *Rhesus*. It is thus a metrical anomaly, and this is the strongest piece of internal evidence against Euripidean authorship. On the other hand, the fragments of Euripides' lost *Phoenix* do contain trochees, and *Phoenix* is securely dated before 425. The forty iambic lines preserved show a resolution rate of only 2.5 per cent. The conclusion must be that Euripides, while he made a habit of using trochees only in his late period, did use them occasionally long before.

The kind of scene which would call for trochees (the "meter of running") is precisely the kind of scene where we find trochees in *Rhesus*: a scene of activity, the scene where Odysseus and Diomedes are caught by the Chorus (ll. 683–91). In general, the characteristics of this play, material and metrical alike, its rapid, realistic action, its failure to find a central hero or a central dramatic problem, can plausibly be explained by the fact that its author did what the dramatic instinct of the fifth century said he should not: he made a book of the *Iliad* into a drama, but the story did better as an episode in epic than as a self-contained tragic action.

This author may not have been Euripides. If he was not, it by no means follows that the play belongs to the fourth century. Some minor poet of the late fifth is as good a guess.

Against the negative evidence, we should set the testimony of Crates that this is an early work by Euripides. This is evidence too, and it is supported by much that is in the play: the character of Odysseus, the messengers' speeches, the combined lament, explanation, and prediction of the Muse (why doesn't she have a name?), and especially the way in which, while reproaching Athene for ingratitude, she contrives to glorify Athens. This is a regular bit of Euripidean *sophia*.

Scholars will continue to doubt, and scholars who honestly doubt must speak their minds. I now believe that *Rhesus* is the work of Euripides and probably done before 440 B.C.

CHARACTERS

Chorus of Trojan guards

Hector

Aeneas

Dolon

Shepherd

Rhesus, king of the Thracians

Odysseus

Diomedes

Athene

Alexander (Paris)

Charioteer of Rhesus

Muse, mother of Rhesus

The manuscripts as usual do not distinguish between the lines spoken or sung by the Chorus as a group and those to be spoken by the Leader alone. In other translations I have followed the text without trying to discriminate. Here, however, the Leader seems to me to have a more definite actor's part then elsewhere in extant tragedy, especially at the beginning. Lines 7–10, for example, should be spoken by a single actor, not by a group; and the speaker must be the officer or non-com in charge of the detail, who is *also* the Leader heading the Chorus. I have therefore used my judgment in guessing where lines are to be given to the Leader and where they should be given to the Chorus.

RHESUS

SCENE: *The Trojan position on the plain between the city and the shore. It is late at night. Hector lies asleep on a pile of leaves with other Trojans asleep around him. Enter, in haste, the Chorus of sentries, headed by an officer or corporal of the guard (the Chorus Leader)*

Leader

Go find where Hector is sleeping. Ho there,
is any of the king's bodyguard awake,
or his armor-bearers?
There is a fresh report he must hear
from those who keep this quarter of the night's   5
guard duty for the entire army.

(Shaking Hector.)

Sit up, or lean your head on your arm;
unclose your lids. Open your keen eyes.
Rise now from the piled leaves of your bed,
Hector. A report. You must hear it.   10

Hector

Who speaks? Enemy or friend? What is
the word? But speak.
Who comes here out of the night to find
where I sleep? Declare.

Leader

Sentries of the army.

Hector

                      What troubles you so?   15

Leader

Never fear.

Hector

            Not I.
What is it? A night raid?

Leader

No, not that.

Hector

Then why
have you left your post to come here and waken
the camp, unless we must form by night?
Do you realize that the Argive spears   20
are there, close by
where we sleep this night in our armor?

Leader

Arm, arm, Hector, and run to where
the allied forces lie sleeping.
Wake them, tell them to take their spears in their hands.   25

(*To various members of the Chorus.*)

You, send true men to run to your company.
You there, put the curb chains on your horses.
Someone go to Panthoüs' son
or Europa's, lord of the Lycian men. Who will?
Where are those who are in charge
of sacrifices?   30
Or the light-armed captains?
Where are the Phrygian archers?
Archers! Have your hornbows strung, quickly.

Hector

What you report seems partly alarm,
partly to be comfort. All is confusion.   35
What is this? Has the whiplash of Cronian Pan
struck you to shivering panic? Speak, say,
what *are* you reporting? You have talked a great deal
without telling me one thing clearly.   40

Leader

The Argive army has lit its fires,
Hector, all through the darkness.

The positions of their ships are clear in the firelight.
But all their army has gathered in darkness
by Agamemnon's shelter, noisily.   45
They must wish to consult, to take
counsel, since never before was this sea-borne army
so utterly routed. Therefore
I, to forestall anything that may happen,
came to report it, so that   50
you will not say I failed to do my duty.

Hector

Good. You are timely, though you come to us in alarm.
I see these people mean to row away by night,
quietly, when I cannot see them, and make good
their flight. I know exactly what their night fires mean.   55
O God, you robbed me, robbed the lion of his spoil.
All prospered, till you halted me before I swept
the Argive army to destruction with this spear.
For if the flaring lanterns of the sun had not
shut down against us, I would never have stayed my spear   60
in its fortune, until I had fired their ships, and made my way
through their camp, killing Achaeans with this murderous hand.
I myself was all ready to keep up the fight,
to use the darkness and the powerful hand of god.
But these diviners, these educated men who know   65
the mind of heaven, persuaded me to wait for day.
Thus no Achaean (they said) would be missed on land.
But will they wait to be carefully slaughtered? No,
not they. The runaway slave is a great man by night.
Come, then. We must pass the order to our men, at once.   70
Have them wake and put on the armor that lies by.
So the Achaean, even while he jumps for his ship,
shall be stabbed in the back and drench the ladderways
with blood. And the survivors can be caught, and tied,
and learn to work the wheat fields in our land of Troy.   75

Leader

Too quick, Hector. You act before you understand.
We are not certain yet that they are running away.

Hector

For what cause did the Argives light their fires?

Leader

I do not know. I am suspicious of the whole matter.

Hector

If you fear this, you would be afraid of anything.   80

Leader

The enemy never lit fires like this before.

Hector

They never fled in such an awful rout before.

Leader

Yes. It was your work. Now consider what comes next.

Hector

There is only one order to give: arm and fight the enemy.

Leader

Here comes Aeneas in great haste   85
of foot, as one who has news for his friends to hear.

(Enter Aeneas.)

Aeneas

Hector, why has the night-guard of the camp come here
to where you were quartered? Is it panic? Here is talk
going on at night, and all the army is disturbed.

Hector

On with your armor quick, Aeneas.   90

Aeneas

                              Yes? What for?
Has someone come in to report the enemy
have made a surprise attack upon us in the dark?

Hector

No, no, they are withdrawing. They are boarding their ships.

Aeneas

And what good reason do you have to believe this?

Hector

Their watch fires are illuminating all the night,   95
and I believe they will not wait until the dawn
but burn them so that by their light they can escape
on their well benched ships, to leave this country and go home.

Aeneas

What will you do to stop them, then? Why are you armed?

Hector

To fall upon them as they flee and board their ships,   100
to charge with our spears against them, and hit hard.
It would be shame, and more than shame, sheer cowardice,
to let them, when they did us so much harm, escape
without a fight, when God has given them to our hands.

Aeneas

I wish you could make plans as well as you can fight.   105
But so it is: the same man cannot well be skilled
in everything; each has his special excellence,
and yours is fighting, and it is for others to make good plans,
not you. You heard how the Achaeans had lit their fires
and hope roused you to wish to lead the army on   110
across their deep moats in the time of night. Yet see,
suppose you do cross over the ditch, despite its depth,

and meet an enemy not withdrawing from our coast
as you think, but standing with spears faced to your attack,
you will have no free way to escape if they defeat you. 115
How will a beaten army cross the palisades?
How will your charioteers drive over the embankments
without smashing the axles of their chariots?
Then, even if you win, they have Achilles in reserve.
He will not sit by while you fire their ships, he will 120
not let you prey on the Achaeans, as you hope.
The man is hot, and he has massive strength of hand.
No, better, let us hold our army out of the way
of hard strokes; let them sleep at peace upon their shields;
but send one volunteer to scout the enemy. 125
So I think best. Then, if they really are in flight,
we can advance in force upon the Argive host.
But if this burning of their fires leads to some trick,
our scout will inform us what they are doing.
Then take our measures. This, my lord, is what I urge. 130

Chorus

This is what I think best. Change your mind and accept it.
I do not like it when the general uses power that is
unsure. What could be better
than that a swift-paced man should go to spy on their ships,
from close, and see what it means 135
when our enemies have fires burning where their prows are
beached?

Hector

Have your way, then, since this is approved by all. Go, you,
and quiet our allies, let them sleep, since the whole army
might well be restless, hearing how we consult at night.
I will send a man to spy upon the enemy, 140
and if we find out that there is some stratagem,
you shall hear all, Aeneas, and be called to plan
with us; but if it is flight and they are casting off,

be ready for action when you hear the trumpet speak;
because I will not wait for you, I shall be there   145
among the Argives and their cables, now, tonight.

Aeneas

Send him with all speed. Now your plan is sound. And if
the need comes for it, I will be as bold as you.

                                                    (*Exit.*)

Hector

Is there a Trojan, then, present at this council,
who volunteers to spy upon the Argive ships?   150
Who is there who would have his country in his debt?
Who speaks? I cannot, by myself, do everything
that must be done to help our city and our friends.

Dolon

I will do it. I willingly undertake this cast
of hazard. I will go and scout the Argive ships   155
and listen to everything they plan to do and bring
word back. On such conditions I accept the task.

Hector

You are well named, my crafty Dolon, and you love
your city well. Your father's house was bright in name
before. Now you have made it twice as bright.   160

Dolon

It is good to work and fight, but when I do, it also
is good to be rewarded. For in every work
a reward added makes the pleasure twice as great.

Hector

True. I will not deny that what you say is fair.
Name your price. Anything except my royal power.   165

Dolon

I do not want your royal power, nor to rule a city.

Hector

Marry a daughter of Priam. Be my brother-in-law.

Dolon

I think it best not to marry above my station.

Hector

I have gold to give, if that is what you will be asking.

Dolon

We have it at home. We do not lack for anything.   170

Hector

What would you have out of the treasures of Ilium?

Dolon

Nothing. Catch the Achaeans, and then grant my gift.

Hector

I shall. But do not ask for the leaders of their fleet.

Dolon

Kill them. I will not ask for Menelaus' life.

Hector

It is not the son of Oïleus you are asking me for?   175

Dolon

Those well-bred hands would never work well in the fields.

Hector

Is there any Achaean you would have alive, for ransom?

Dolon

I told you before. We have gold aplenty in our house.

Hector

Well, you shall come and take your own pick from the spoils.

Dolon

Take them, and nail them on the houses of the gods.   180

Hector

What prize greater than such things can you ask me for?

Dolon

The horses of Achilles.
                    Since I risk my life
on dice the gods throw, it must be for a high stake.

Hector

Ah. You are my rival, for I want those horses too.
They are immortal, born of an immortal strain,   185
who bear the fighting son of Peleus. The king
of the sea, Poseidon, broke them once and tamed them and gave
them to Peleus, so the story goes. Yet I have raised
your hopes, and I will not be false. I give you them:
Achilles' horses, a great possession for your house.   190

Dolon

I thank you. Thus my courage shall have a reward
that will outshine all others in the land of Troy.
But you should not be jealous. There is much besides
for you, our best and greatest, to take glory in.

(*Hector retires to the rear of the stage and rests.*)

Chorus

High is the venture, high are the honors you hope to capture.   195
Blessed will your name be called if you win. For here
is glorious work to be done.
It would have been bold to marry into the house of our kings.
May the gods grant that Right's eyes be on you,
as men now grant that all you deserve shall be yours.   200

Dolon

I am ready, once I have gone inside my house
and put upon my body the necessary gear.
From there, I shall take my way against the Argive ships.

Chorus

What costume will you wear in place of what you have on?

Dolon

One suited to my venture and my stealthy way.   205

Chorus

Some cleverness is to be learned from the clever man.
Tell me then, how do you mean to have your body arrayed?

Dolon

I shall put a wolfskin upon my back, fitted
so that the grinning jaws of the beast are on my head,
then, with the forepaws on my hands and the hind feet   210
upon my legs, shall imitate the four-foot tread
of the wolf, to puzzle the enemy who track me there
beside the ditch and by the bows of the beached ships.
Then when I reach the lonely stretch where no one is
I shall go upright. Thus my strategy is planned.   215

Chorus

May Hermes, son of Maia, bring you there and bring
you back, since Hermes is the friend of slippery men.
You know your business. All you need now is good luck.

Dolon

I shall come safely back, but kill Odysseus first
and bring his head to you, to give you solid grounds   220
for saying Dolon won through to the Argive ships.
Or maybe Diomedes—but my hand will not
be bloodless when, before the day breaks, I come home.

                                                    (*Exit.*)

Chorus

Lord of Thymbraeum, lord of Delos, who stand
upright in the Lycian shrine,   225
Apollo, O shining presence, come with your bow
armed, come in the night,
lead, preserve, and guide on his way this man
of battles, lend your strength to Dardanus' children,   230
O power complete, who long ago
founded the walls of Troy.

Grant that he reach their shipsteads and come to spy
on the spread army of Greece
and turn and make his way back to the house of his father
and the sacred hearth, in Troy;   235
and grant, some day, he may mount the Phthian horse-chariot,
after our chief has smashed the war strength of Achaea,
and win the gift the sea god gave   240
once to Peleus, son of Aeacus.

Yes, for he alone dared go down to spy on their ships
for our land and people. I admire
his courage; for indeed few
are found brave when the city   245
is a ship riding a hard
storm on the open
water. There is still manhood alive in Phrygia   250
and valor left still in her spears.
What Mysian is there who holds
scorn that I fight beside him?

What shall that man of Achaea be whom our stalking killer
will spear among the shelters as he goes
on fours in the pace of a lurking   255
beast? Might it be Menelaus!
Or might he kill Agamemnon
and bring the head back

as a gloomy gift for the arms of his evil sister   260
by marriage, Helen. For he
it was led the thousand ships
and the army here against Troy.

> (*Enter hastily a shepherd. As he speaks, Hector
> rises and comes forward.*)

Shepherd

My lord, I hope I can always bring my masters news
as good as what I bring you now, for you to hear.   265

Hector

What crude creatures these yokels are. They have no sense.
You think it fitting to report about the flocks
to the armed nobility? You have no business here.
Do you not know where my house is, or my father's throne?
Go there for your announcement that the sheep are well.   270

Shepherd

We herdsmen are crude creatures, I will not say no.
Nevertheless, I am the bringer of good news.

Hector

Will you stop trying to tell me about what goes on
in the farmyard? We have spears and fighting on our hands.

Shepherd

But it is just such matters I report to you.   275
There is a man, with strength of thousands at his back,
who comes to fight for our country at your side.

Hector

Where are the native plains that he has emptied of men?

Shepherd

Thrace; and his father is called Strymon.

Hector

Do you mean
that Rhesus has set foot on Trojan soil?   280

Shepherd

You have it. So saved me half of what I had to say.

Hector

How did he lose the carriage road on the broad plains
to wander through the herds on Ida's mountainside?

Shepherd

I do not know exactly. I can guess at it.
It is no small thing to bring an army through the night   285
when you know the plain is full of enemies in arms.
We countrymen, who live where Ida runs to rock,
and plant our hearth on the bare ground, took alarm, as he
came through the oak wood with its animals in the night.
Because this army of the Thracians streamed along   290
with great clamor, and we, terror-stricken, ran away
to the high pastures, fearing some Argives had come
on a plundering expedition and to rob your folds.
But then our ears made out their language; it was not
anything Greek, and now we were no more afraid.   295
I went and stood before the pathway of their king,
hailed him, and questioned him aloud in Thracian speech:
"Who rides as general here, and of what father called
comes he in arms to fight by Priam's citadel?"
Then, having heard answers to all I wished to know,   300
I stood and watched. There I saw Rhesus like a god
upright behind his horses in the Thracian car.
The golden balance of a yoke inclosed the necks
of his young horses, and these were whiter than snow.
The buckler on his shoulders glowed with beaten plates   305
of gold, and as upon a goddess' aegis, the bronze
face of a gorgon on the horses' frontlet shields

glared, and with bells beat out a clashing sound of fear.
I could not reckon on an abacus the count
of all their army, so innumerable did it seem,   310
horsemen in numbers, numerous squads of buckler men,
many archers with unfeathered arrows, and, besides,
the light troops, in their Thracian costume, followed with them.
Such is the man who comes to fight for Troy. Neither
by flight, nor yet by standing to him with the spear,   315
will Peleus' son Achilles find escape from death.

Leader

When the gods change and stand behind the citizens,
our depressed fortune climbs uphill, and wins success.

Hector

Now that my spear is fortunate, and Zeus is on
our side, we shall be finding that we have many friends.   320
We can do without them. We want none who did not fight
our perils, past now, when the driving God of War
blew big upon our city's ship and wrecked our sails.
Rhesus has shown what kind of friend he is to Troy.
He is here for the feasting, but he was not there   325
with spear in hand to help the huntsmen catch the game.

Leader

Your grievance and complaint of friends is just. And yet,
accept those who, of their free will, will fight for us.

Hector

We have saved Ilium this long time. We are enough.

Leader

Are you so sure you have the enemy beaten now?   330

Hector

I am so sure. God's daylight, which is near, will show.

Leader

Look to the future. God often reverses fortunes.

Hector

I hate it in friends when they come too late to help.   333
As for this man, since he is here, let him be here   336
as a stranger guest at our table, but as no fighting man.   337
He has lost all the kind feelings of the sons of Troy.   338

Leader

Spurn allies, lord, and you gain peril and lose love.   334

Shepherd

If the enemy only saw him they would be afraid.   335

Hector

                                    (*To Chorus.*)

You urge me faithfully.

                                    (*To Shepherd.*)

                    You have given a timely report.   339
So, for the sake of what the messenger has said,   340
let golden-armored Rhesus come as our ally.

Chorus

Adrasteia: Necessity: Zeus'
daughter! Keep bad luck from my mouth.
For I will speak what is in my heart.
All I wish shall be spoken.   345
You are here, child of the River,
here, at long last now in the court of Friendship,
and welcome, since it was long, before
the Muse your mother and the grand-channeled
River-God sent you to help us.   350

This was Strymon, who with the Muse
melodious, in the clear shining
and watery swirl of their embrace

begot your youth and glory.
You come, a Zeus resplendent   355
for show, driving behind your dappled horses.
Now, O my country, my Phrygia,
now, with gods' will, we can claim the aid
of Zeus himself, Liberator.

Will it ever happen again that our ancient Troy   360
will know the day-long revelries,
the love pledge and companionship,
the strumming on the lyres and the wine cups circling,
passed to the right, in sweet contention,
while on the open water the sons
of Atreus make for Sparta,   365
gone from the shores of Ilium.
O friend, could it only be
that with hand and spear you could do
this before you leave us.

O come, appear, lift and flourish your golden buckler,   370
slant it across the eyes
of Peleus' son, over
the split chariot-rail, feint with your feet, then
cast the twin javelins. None
who stands against you shall dance   375
ever again on the level lands
of Argive Hera. He shall die
here, by a Thracian death, a welcome
weight on this land, which will take him.

Great King, he comes, O great King.

(*Rhesus enters, with some of his following.*)

Gallant, O Thrace,   380
is this youngling you bred, a monarch to behold.
See the great force on his gold-armored body,
hear the brave noise of his clashing bells

that jangle on the shield rim.
A god, O Troy, a god, a real Ares   385
is this stallion sired by the singing muse
and Strymon, who comes to inspire you.

Rhesus

Great son of a great father, despot of this land,
O Hector, hail. On this late day I greet you,
and greet the good success that finds you so advanced   390
against the enemy's fortress. I am here to help
you knock their walls to rubble and to burn their ships.

Hector

O son of a melodious mother, one of the Nine,
and Strymon, the River of Thrace: it is my way
always to speak the truth. I have no diplomacy.   395
Long, long ago you should have come to help our struggle.
For all you have done, Troy could have fallen to Greek arms.
This should not be.
You will not say it was because your friends never called you
that you did not come, and did not help, and paid no heed.   400
What herald or what aged representatives
did not reach you, to entreat you to our city's help?
What honorable gifts did we not send? For all
you did, you might as well have thrown us to the Greeks,
though you and we are non-Greek, one Barbarian blood.   405
Yet it was I who with this hand made you so great
and lord of Thrace, though you were but a small baron
before I swept Pangaeum and Paeonia,
fought with the Thracian bravest face to face, and broke
their lines of bucklers, made slaves of their people, turned 410
them over to you. You owe us much. You have spurned it
and to your friends in distress come with late relief.
Yet here are others, who are not our kin by blood,
who came long ago, and some of them have fallen and lie
buried in their mounds, who greatly kept faith with our city, 415

while others, in their armor, by their chariot teams,
have stood whatever cold winds or thirsty heat the god
sends, and still do endure it, without
sleeping, as you did, snug beneath the covers.
There, you may know that Hector speaks his mind.   420
I have my grievance, and I tell you to your face.

Rhesus

I am another such as you. I have a path
straight through arguments. I too have no diplomacy.
But I have been hurt more at the heart than you, more vexed
and shamed, not to be here in your country.   425
But see. There is a land neighbor to mine, its people
are Scythian, and as I was about to keep appointment
at Ilium, these attacked me. I had reached the shores
of the Euxine Sea, to put my Thracian army across,
and there the ground was sopped with Scythian blood, and
    Thracian   430
too, as the spearwork made commingled slaughter.
Such were the accidents that kept me from my march
to Troy's plain and my arrival as your ally.
Once I had beaten them, made hostages of their children,
and set a yearly tribute to be brought to us,   435
I crossed the sea gate with my ships, went on by land
over the intervening country, and so am here;
not, as you claim, because I stayed in comfort, not
because I slept at leisure in my golden house.
For I know well, I have endured them, those stiff winds   440
of ice that sweep Paeonia and the Thracian Sea.
Sleepless, and in this armor, I have come through these
and come to you behind my time, but timely still,
for here is the tenth summer of your years of war,
and *you* have made no progress, but day after day   445
you throw your dice against the hazard of Argive arms;
one single day of sunlight is enough for *me*
to storm their walls and burst upon their mooring-steads

and kill the Achaeans. On the next day after that
I am off for home, having disposed of your whole war.   450
Not one of your people needs to lift a single shield.
I will deal with these vaunted Achaeans and their spears,
and destroy them, even though I came behind my time.

Chorus

Hail, hail,
welcome your cry, welcome, you come from Zeus, only I pray   455
that Zeus keep away
the invincible Spirit of Envy from cursing your words.
For what man from Argos
did the sea-armament bring, before   460
or now, stronger than you? Say how
could even Achilles endure your spear?
How could Ajax endure it?
If I could only see, my lord, only see that day
when your spear hand   465
is bloody with retribution.

Rhesus

Now for my too-long absence I will make amends
thus (but may Adrasteia not resent my words):
when we have liberated this city of yours and when
you have chosen first spoils and devoted them to the gods,   470
I am willing to sail with you against the Argives, storm
and ravage the whole land of Hellas with our spears.
So let them learn what it is like to be attacked.

Hector

If I could only get rid of my present troubles
and rule a peaceful city as I did before   475
I would be very grateful to the gods.
As for the Argive country and the Greek domain,
they are not so easy to devastate as you seem to think.

Rhesus

    Do they not say the greatest of the Greeks are here?

Hector

    They are great enough for me. I want no more.   480

Rhesus

    Then, once we have killed these, have we not done everything?

Hector

    Do not plan for ventures before finishing what's at hand.

Rhesus

    You seem content to be acted on, not to act.

Hector

    I have my own kingdom here, and it is large.
    Now, whether you want the left wing, or the right,   485
    or to be among the central allies, take your choice,
    and plant your shields, station your army where you wish.

Rhesus

    My wish, Hector, is to fight the enemy alone;
    but if you think it shame to take no hand in burning
    their beached ships, an end for which you fought so long,   490
    set me face to face with Achilles and his men.

Hector

    It is not possible to set your eager spears
    against him.

Rhesus

              The story was he sailed to Troy.

Hector

    He sailed. He is here. But angry
    with their generals, and takes no part in the fighting.   495

Rhesus

Who is most famous in their army after him?

Hector

Ajax, I think, is just as good, and Tydeus' son
Diomedes. Then there is that talker, that big mouth,
Odysseus, but his heart is brave enough, who has done
more damage to our country than any single man.   500
He it was who crept in the night to Athene's shrine
and stole her image and took it to the Argive ships.
There was a time the Argives sent him to scout us,
and in a beggarman's miserable outfit, disguised,
he got inside our walls and did us great mischief.   505
For he killed the sentries and the gate guards and got free
away. Constantly he is observed, under cover
by the Thymbraean altar, near the city, watching
his chance. A wicked planner, always on our hands.

Rhesus

Why, no true man of spirit deigns to kill his man   510
by stealth. One should go forward and attack direct.
This man you speak of, crouching in thievish ambuscades
and scheming stratagems, this man I will seize alive,
impale him through the back where the road goes out the gates,
and leave him there to feed the vultures.   515
That is the kind of death that such a man should die
for being a simple brigand and a temple robber.

Hector

Well, it is night now, and time for you to bivouac.
I will show you your place, apart from where the rest
of the army is stationed. There your men can spend the night.   520
Should you want anything, the watchword is "Phoebus."
Learn it. Remember. Tell it to your Thracian force.

(To the Chorus.)

Now, you must go out in advance of our position,
keep a sharp watch, and be on the lookout for Dolon
who scouted the ships, for, if he is still alive,   525
he must be almost back now to the Trojan camp.

*(Exeunt all principals. The Chorus have the stage to themselves.
There is some business of waking men who lie asleep on the
ground or calling to imaginary persons off stage.)*

Leader

Whose is the watch now? Who relieves
mine? The early constellations
are setting. The Pleiades' sevenfold course
rides high, and the Eagle soars in the center of heaven.   530
Wake. What keeps you? Wake
from your sleep, to your watch.
Do you not see how the moon shines?
Dawn is near, dawn   535
is breaking now, here is the star
that runs before it.

Who was announced for the first watch?

First Soldier

Coroebus, they say, Mygdon's son.

Leader

Who was after that?

First Soldier

                                    The Paeonian force   540
relieved the Cilicians. Mysians relieved us.

Leader

Then is it not time to go wake the Lycians
and relieve, take the fifth
watch, in our turn, as allotted?   545

Second Soldier

I hear. But perched above Simois
the nightingale,
the own–child–slayer in vociferous chant
sings her murderous marriage, sings her song and her sorrow.　　550

Third Soldier

The flocks are pasturing on Ida
now. I can hear the night-murmuring
call of the shepherd's pipe.

Fourth Soldier

Sleep is a magic on my eyes.
It comes sweetest　　　　　　　　　　　　　　　　　555
to the lids about dawn.

Fifth Soldier

Why is the scout not here, that one
Hector sent to spy on their ships?

Sixth Soldier

I fear for him. He is long gone.

Fifth Soldier

Might he have stumbled into an ambush　　　　　　560
and been killed?

Sixth Soldier

He might. It is to be feared.

Leader

My orders are to go wake the Lycians
and relieve, take the fifth
watch, in our turn, as allotted.

(*The Chorus file out, leaving the stage empty. Then
enter, furtively, Odysseus and Diomedes.*)

Odysseus

    Diomedes, did you hear? Or was it a noise without   565
    meaning that falls on my ears? Some clash of armor?

Diomedes

    It was nothing, the jangle of iron on the harness
    against the chariot rails. But I was frightened too,
    at first, when I heard the clanking of the harness.

Odysseus

    Be careful. You might run into their sentries in the dark.   570

Diomedes

    I will watch how I step despite the darkness.

Odysseus

    If you do wake anyone, do you know what their watchword is?

Diomedes

    I know it. It's "Phoebus." Dolon told me.

Odysseus

    Look!
    Here are some bivouacs of the enemy. But empty.

Diomedes

    Dolon spoke of this too. He said Hector should be sleeping   575
    here. And it is for Hector that this sword is drawn.

Odysseus

    What can it mean? Is there an ambush set up somewhere?

Diomedes

    He may have gone to work some stratagem against us.

Odysseus

    Hector is bold, very bold, now that he is winning.

Diomedes

What shall we do now, Odysseus? We hoped to find   580
our man asleep, but we've failed.

Odysseus

We must go back to our mooring-place as quick as we can.
Whatever god it is who grants him his success
is watching over him now. We must not force Fortune.

Diomedes

But should we not look for Aeneas? Or for that Phrygian   585
we hate worst of all, Paris? Cut his head off?

Odysseus

How, without deadly peril, can you find these men
in the dark, and here among our enemies?

Diomedes

But it is shameful to go back to the Argive ships
without doing our enemies the least damage.   590

Odysseus

How can you say you have done no damage? Did we not kill
Dolon, who scouted our ships? Do we not carry his armor
here, our spoils? Do you think you can rout their whole army?

Diomedes

You are right. Let us go back. May we only succeed!

*(The voice of Athene is heard, but, though visible to the
audience, she is not visible to the characters.)*

Athene

Where are you going? Why do you leave the Trojan camp   595
biting your very hearts for disappointed spite
because the god will not allow you to kill their Hector
or their Paris? Have you not heard of the ally,

Rhesus, who has come to Troy in no mean circumstance?
For if he survives this night and is alive tomorrow,   600
not even Achilles, and not Ajax with his spear,
can keep him from destroying all the Argive fleet,
smashing, demolishing your walls and storming in
to fight with level spears.
Kill him, and all is won. Let Hector bivouac   605
in peace, nor try to murder him.
His death shall come, but it shall come from another hand.

Odysseus

Athene, mistress, for I recognized your voice
and way of speaking that I know so well, and know
how you are always with me and watch over me,   610
tell me, where is this man sleeping whom you bid us
attack? Where is his station in the Trojan camp?

Athene

He is camped right here and has not joined the main army.
Hector gave him this place to sleep, outside the lines,
until this night passes and day comes, and by him   615
are picketed the horses from the Thracian
chariots, so white that you can see them through the dark
gleaming, as if they were the wings of swans on water.
Kill their master and bring these home to your camp,
spoils of surpassing splendor, for no place on earth   620
contains a team of chariot horses such as these.

Odysseus

Diomedes, yours be the work of killing Thracians—
or let me do it, and you look after the horses.

Diomedes

I will do the killing, you manage the horses.
You are the experienced one, the quick improviser.   625
One ought to place a man where he can do most good.

Athene

    Alexander is here, I see him, coming our way
    in haste. He must have heard from some of the guards
    confused rumors about the presence of enemies.

Diomedes

    Does he have others with him or is he by himself?   630

Athene

    He's alone. He seems to be making for where Hector sleeps,
    so he can report to him the presence of spies in the camp.

Diomedes

    Well, should he not be killed and his account settled?

Athene

    No. You must not go beyond what has been destined for you.
    There is no authority for you to kill this man.   635
    You came here, bringing their destined death to certain others.
    Do it. Dispatch. Now to this man I shall pretend
    I am his Cyprian ally, standing beside him
    in all perils. I'll hold him here with rotten lies.
    This I have said. But though my victim stands close by   640
    he's heard and knows nothing of what's in store for him.

      (Diomedes and Odysseus vanish as Alexander [Paris] appears.)

Paris

    Hector, my general, my brother, Hector I say,
    are you sleeping? How can you sleep? Waken, will you?
    Here is some enemy got close inside our lines;
    someone has come to rob us, or to spy on us.   645

Athene

    Fear not. Here is your faithful Aphrodite
    watching over you. Your war is my war. I do not forget
    your favor and your kindness to me. I am grateful,

and now, to your Trojan army in its high success
I come, bringing a friend and mighty man of war,   650
the Thracian, child of that divine maker of melodies,
the Muse herself; the River Strymon is named his father.

Paris

Always you are in truth the good friend of my city
and me. I think the best thing I ever did
in my life was to judge you first and win you to my city.   655
What brings me here—there are wild rumors flying about
among the sentries, nothing clear. Achaean spies
said to be among us. One man reports but has not seen them;
another saw them coming but knows nothing else
about it. This is why I came to Hector's quarters.   660

Athene

Never fear. There's nothing wrong in the camp.
Hector is gone to give the Thracians a place to sleep.

Paris

I trust you. I always believe what you say. I'll go
and keep my station, free of this anxiety.

Athene

Go, for your interests are always on my mind,   665
and all my purpose is to see my friends succeed.
Oh, you will learn soon how I shall take care of you.

(Paris goes. Athene calls inward to Odysseus and Diomedes.)

You two, in there. You are too bold. You, I am calling
you, son of Laertes, put your sharp sword away.
Our Thracian captain's down.   670
We have his horses, but the enemy are aware
and coming at you. Now is the time for speed, speed,
to run for where the ships are moored. What keeps you?
The enemy are upon you. Save your lives.

*(From one side Odysseus and Diomedes, from the other the
Chorus of Trojan sentries, come cautiously on,
and run into each other, to their mutual
surprise, as Athene vanishes.)*

First Soldier

There they go, there!

Second Soldier

Shoot, shoot.

675

Third Soldier

Spear them.

Fourth Soldier

Who is it? Look! That's the man I mean.

Fifth Soldier

They have come to rob us in the night, and they have roused the
camp.

Leader

This way all.

680

Sixth Soldier

Here they are. We have them fast.

Leader

What's your regiment? Where do you come from? Who are you?

Odysseus

Nothing for you to know. You have done an evil day's work.
You shall die.

Leader

Tell me the watchword, will you, before you get this spear stuck
through your chest.

Odysseus

Stop. There's no danger.

Leader

Bring him here. Now, everyone, strike him.

Odysseus

Was it you killed Rhesus?

Leader

No. You tried to kill him. We'll kill *you!*

Odysseus

Hold hard everyone.

Leader

We will not.

Odysseus

Hold. You must not kill a friend.

Leader

What's the watchword?

Odysseus

Phoebus.

Leader

I acknowledge it. Down spears all.
Do you know where the men have got to?

Odysseus

Yes, I saw them go this way.

> (*He points. As the Leader and his men start in
> that direction, Odysseus and Diomedes
> slip out on the opposite side.*)

Leader

On their trail, then, everyone.

Seventh Soldier

                Should we raise a general alarm?   690

Leader

No. It would be bad to disturb our friends with an alarm in the
night.

        (All go off, but almost immediately begin to
        return, singing the following ode as
        they re-enter severally.)

Chorus

Who was the man who was here?
Who is it so hardy that he shall boast
that he escaped my hand?
Where shall I find him now?   695
What shall I think he can be,
that man who came on fearless foot through the dark
across the stations of our ranks and our guards?
Some Thessalian
or some dweller in a seaside Locrian city?   700
One whose living is made on the scattered islands?
Who was it? Where did he come from? What country?
Which god does he acknowledge as god supreme?

First Soldier

Was this the work of Odysseus after all? Or whose?

Second Soldier

If we are to judge by past deeds, who else?   705

First Soldier

You think so?

Second Soldier

          I must do.

First Soldier

He has been bold against us?

Third Soldier
  Bold? Who? Whom are you praising?

First Soldier
                              Odysseus.

Third Soldier
  Never praise him, that thief, that treacherous fighter.

Chorus
  He came once before   710
  into our citadel, bleary eyed
  and huddled in a disguise
  of rags, his sword hand
  hidden under his clothes,
  begging his bread he crept in, a wretched vagrant,   715
  dirty, unkempt, foul.
  and much evil he spoke
  against the royal house of the sons of Atreus
  as if he had hated all the lords of their host.
  I wish he had died, died as he deserved   720
  before he ever set foot on the Phrygian shore.

Leader
  Whether it was Odysseus or not, I am afraid.
  We are the picket, and Hector will hold us to blame.

First Soldier
  With what charge?

Leader
  With curses.

First Soldier
  For doing what? What do you fear?   725

Leader
  Because they got through us.

« 38 »

First Soldier
Who did?

Leader

Those men who got into the Phrygian camp tonight.

Thracian Charioteer (within)

Oh god. Disaster.

Leader

Listen!
Silence. Keep your places all. Perhaps someone is in our nets.   730

Charioteer

Halloo, help!
Disaster and ruin of the Thracians.

Leader

                                        This is one of our allies
in pain or terror.

Charioteer (entering)

Halloo!
I am hurt, I am done. And you, lord of the Thracians,
how hateful that day you saw Troy,
what an end to your life.   735

Leader

You must be one of our allies, but who? My eyes
fail me in the dark. I cannot clearly make you out.

Charioteer

Where can I find some chief of the Trojans?
Where is Hector himself?
Drowsing somewhere, sleeping under arms?   740
Is there none in command to whom I can report
what happened to us, what someone has done

and got clean away, vanished, leaving plain to see
the hurt he inflicted on the Thracians?

Leader

Some mishap has come to the Thracian force, it seems   745
from what this man says.

Charioteer

The army is shattered, the king is killed
by a traitor's stroke,
and oh, my own wound hurts   750
deep and bleeds. Shall I die? Must both
Rhesus and I be basely killed
in Troy, which we came to help?

Leader

There is no mystery in ill news he reports
now; it is plain that some of our allies are killed.   755

Charioteer

There has been wickedness done here. More than wickedness;
shame too, which makes the evil double its own bulk.
To die with glory, if one has to die at all,
is still, I think, pain for the dier, surely so,
but grandeur left for his survivors, honor for his house.   760
But death to us came senseless and inglorious.
When Hector with his own hand led us to our quarters
and gave us the watchword, we lay down to sleep, worn out
with the fatigue of our long march. No one kept watch
in our contingent for that night, nor were our arms   765
stacked out in order, nor were the goads in place beside
the yokes of the horses, since our king had been assured
that you were masters of the field and your pickets threatened
their anchorage; so we dropped in our tracks, and grossly slept.
Yet my own heart was restless, and I woke again   770
to give some fodder to the horses, thinking we must

harness them for the dawn's fighting, so I heaped their food
lavishly. Now I see two fellows stealing through our camp
in the dim dark, but when I started in their direction
they dodged away and made off.   775
I called out and warned them to stay away from the camp.
I thought some of the allies had gone out to steal
from us.
       No reply.
              I did not give it another thought.
I went back to where I had been, and slept again.
But now there came an apparition to my sleep.   780
Those horses, that I trained and drove as charioteer
at Rhesus' side, I saw them, as one sees in a dream,
but wolves had got astride their backs and rode them now,
and stabbed and gored their backs and rumps with goads, and
    the mares
went wild with terror, bucking and fighting, snorting   785
from flared nostrils.
I started up to drive those savage beasts away
from the mares, for the dream's terror had awakened me.
As I raised my head I heard a moan such as men make
when they die, and a jet of hot fresh blood splashed me. It came 790
from my master, who had been murdered, and died hard.
I leapt upright, but there was no spear in my hand,
and as I looked about and fumbled for a weapon
somebody coming close up slashed me hard in the side
with a sword. I took and felt a cut from the blade   795
that ripped me deep.
I fell on my face. He and the other man seized the team
and car, mounted, galloped away, and escaped.
Ah.
I am faint from my wound, I cannot stand.
I know what happened, for I saw it, but do not   800
understand in what way these men could have been killed
nor what hand killed them. I can guess.
My guess is that our friends were the ones who hurt us.

Leader

> O charioteer of that unfortunate Thracian king,
> do not be angry with us. The enemy did this.   805
> And here is Hector in person, who has heard the news
> and comes, I think, in sympathy for your misfortune.

(*Hector enters hastily.*)

Hector (*to the Chorus*)

> You are responsible for a disaster. How did it happen
> that these marauders sent out by the enemy
> got past you and made havoc in our camp? Disgraceful!   810
> Why did you neither head them off as they came in
> nor catch them as they went out? Someone will pay for this,
> and who but you? I hold you responsible. You had the watch.
> Now they are gone, untouched, and much amused, no doubt,
> with the feebleness of the Trojans, and of me, their leader.   815
> I tell you now—father Zeus be witness to my oath—
> death by flogging or by the headsman's ax awaits you
> for your part in this. Else, say Hector is a weakling.
> Say he is nothing.

Chorus

> No, no!   820
> We came to you, lord, defender of the city, we did,
> we came (it must have been these),
> we told you their fires were burning beside the ships.
> Since then, all through the night's vigil   825
> our eyes have not deadened, they have not slept,
> by the springs of Simois we swear it. O my lord,
> do not be angry with us. None of all this
> that has happened is our fault.
> If again, in the course of time, you prove we have said or done   830
> anything wrong, then bury us
> alive in the ground. We will not protest.

Charioteer (*to Hector*)

You are Barbarian, so are we. Why do you parry
my charge by threatening these men? Why make a Greek
lawyer's speech here?
You did this.

            We Thracians,   835
the wounded and the dead, will not be satisfied
with anyone else. It would take you a long and artful speech
to convince me that you have not been killing your friends.
You coveted those horses. For their sake, you murdered
your own allies, whose coming you had begged so hard.   840
They did come. They are dead. When Paris shamed hospitality
he was better than you—you murderer of your friends and
    helpers.
Never tell me it was one of the Argives
got through to destroy us. Who could slip through the Trojan
    lines
without detection and reach us?   845
You and the whole of the Phrygian army lay between.
Who of your own particular allies is dead,
or wounded, by those enemies you speak of? We
who lay beyond are wounded, some, while others fared worse
and do not look any longer on the light of the sun.   850
I tell you plain. I do not think this was any Achaean.
Who could pick a path through the enemy in the dark
and find where Rhesus lay—unless they were directed
by a god? They would not even know
of his arrival. Your defense is artificial.   855

Hector

We have had the help of our allies through all the time
that the Achaean army has been on our shores,
and not one word of complaint has come from any of them
of ill treatment. You would be our first. I hope
no greed for horses ever makes me kill my friends   860
to get them. This is more of Odysseus. What man else

among the Argives could have planned and done it?
I fear him. The thought, too, racks my mind,
he might have chanced to meet Dolon and killed him. Dolon
has been gone for a long time, and there's no sign of him.   865

Charioteer

I don't know what "Odysseuses" you're talking about.
I do know we're hurt, and it was no enemy did it.

Hector

Since you cannot think otherwise, you must think this.

Charioteer

O land of my fathers, how can I reach you, and there die?

Hector

No dying. Too many have died already.   870

Charioteer

I have lost my masters. Where shall I turn me?

Hector

My own house will take you in and make you well.

Charioteer

How shall the hands of his murderers take care of me?

Hector

This man keeps saying the same thing. He will not stop.

Charioteer

Perish the murderer. I do not mean you,   875
you need not protest. The Spirit of Justice knows who did it.

Hector

Take him up. Help him into my house,
then look after him carefully, so that he will not
be complaining any more.

You go to the forces on the wall,
to Priam and the elders. Tell them it is time   880
to bury these dead beside the highway where it leaves
our city.

> (*Some soldiers [not the Chorus] lift the Thracian*
> *charioteer and carry him out, while others*
> *leave to deliver the last message.*)

Chorus

After our high success, does the god
now change Troy's luck, bring us back, to suffer
new losses? What does he plan?

> (*The Muse appears above, holding in her*
> *arms the body of Rhesus.*)

But see, see,   885
my King, over your head, what goddess
hovers, carrying aloft in her arms
the man lately slain?
A pitiful sight. It fills me with fear.

The Muse

Behold me, Trojans, and fear not. I am the Muse,   890
one of the Nine and prized among the poets, who stand
before you. I have seen the death of my dear son
so sadly slain by the enemy. His killer, treacherous
Odysseus, some day shall be punished as he deserves.

With my own song of mourning   895
I mourn you, my child. Oh, you hurt
your mother when you went
that day to Troy,
a cursed, wretched way.
I would not have had you go, but you went.   900
Your father restrained you, but you broke away.
I mourn you, my child, dear,
dearest head, I mourn you.

Chorus

    I, too, as much as ever one can grieve
    who has no kinship with the dead, grieve for your son.   905

The Muse

    Perish the scion of Oeneus.
    Perish the son of Laertes.
    He made me childless, who had
    the best child in the world.
    Perish the woman who forsook   910
    her Greek home for a Phrygian bed.
    She, dearest son, she is your true destroyer,
    she, who made the unnumbered cities
    empty of the brave.
    Philammon's son, who live and die your many lives   915
    and deaths, you have struck back and wounded me deep,
    O Thamyris.
    Rude violence did all. It brought you down. The quarrel
    of the Muses, too, made me bear this unhappy son;
    for as I waded through the waters of the Strymon,
    the River-God was on me, I was in his arms   920
    and conceived. It was when we Muses, all arrayed
    with instruments, went to the gold-soiled mountain-mass
    of Pangaeus, and the high contest of melody
    with that great Thracian singer, and we blinded him,
    Thamyris, who had vilified our craft of song.   925
    When you were born, in shame over my maidenhood
    and before my sisters, I flung you into the great waters
    of your father, and Strymon gave you into the care
    of no mortals, but the maiden nymphs of his own springs
    who nursed you to perfection and then sent you forth,   930
    child, to be king of Thrace and first of mortal men.
    There in the bloody valors of your land's defense
    I never feared your death.
    Only to Troy I warned you you must never go
    knowing what waited you there, but Hector's embassies   935

and the repeated conclaves of the men of state
persuaded you to move to the defense of friends.

Athene! You alone are guilty of this death.
Odysseus and the son of Tydeus were your agents,
they could have done nothing. Never think I do not know.   940
And yet I and my sister Muses make your Athens
great in our art, and by our presence in the land;
and it was Orpheus, own blood cousin to this man
you have slain, who first instructed your people in the rites
of mystery and secrets revealed; last, it was we   945
the sisters who with Phoebus educated
Musaeus, your great and respected citizen,
so he surpassed our other pupils.
Here is your gratitude. I hold my son in my arms
and mourn him.
                    I need no advocate, Athene.

Chorus

Hector, that Thracian charioteer with his mad charge   950
that we plotted Rhesus' murder is proved wrong.

Hector

I knew that well. It took no divination
to see the hand of Odysseus in this warrior's death.
And as for my part, when I saw the Greek army camped
on our shores, what should I do but send my heralds out   955
to our allies and ask them to come and help?
I sent heralds. This man was in my debt. He came to help.
But do not think I am unmoved by his death.
I am even ready to make him a great funeral mound
and burn the glory of innumerable robes.   960
He was my friend. He came to help. His loss is mourned.

The Muse

Rhesus will not go to the black meadow in the earth.
So much at least I claim from the infernal bride,

the daughter of Demeter, goddess of the fields,
that she remit his life. She is in debt to me   965
for her ordaining of the Orphics' revelations.
For me he will be as one dead, with no more light
in his eyes, for the rest of time. He will not come again
to where he looks upon his mother any more.
Hidden deep in the caves among the silver mines   970
he shall live on, a human Spirit underground,
where Bacchus' medium under the Pangaean horn
is housed, a holy god to the initiate.
The load of grief that I must bear is lighter
than that of the sea goddess. Her son too must die.   975
I with my sisters first shall dirge your death, my son,
then mourn Achilles, on Thetis' day of sorrow.
Pallas, who killed you, cannot save him.
Apollo's quiver holds the shaft which means his death.

O making of children, hapless work, sorrow of mankind,   980
the man who reasons well
will live his life through childless and not risk the children
whom some day he must bury.

(The Muse disappears.)

Leader

Rhesus is in his mother's hands, and she will mourn him.
Hector, your work lies now before you. It is dawn.   985
It is time. What would you have us do?

Hector

About your business. Tell the allies to arm with speed,
and yoke their horses to the chariots,
then, when full armed, await the call of the Tyrrhenian
trumpet. For I am confident we can overrun
the camp and walls of the Achaeans, fire their ships,   990
and that this sunlight that begins to climb
brings us of Troy our day of liberty.

Leader

Obey the King. Let us march, well armed,
in good order, give the word
to the allies. Who knows? The god who is on our side
might grant us the victory.

995

Paris

Always you are in truth the good friend of my city
and me. I think the best thing I ever did

and all my purpose is to see my friends succeed.
Oh, you will learn soon how I shall take care of you.

(*Paris goes. Athene calls inward to Odysseus and Diomedes.*)

THE SUPPLIANT WOMEN

Translated by Frank Jones

INTRODUCTION TO
THE SUPPLIANT WOMEN

THIS play, which may be dated between 420 and 415 B.C., deals with the aftermath of the war stirred up against Eteocles, a son of Oedipus, by his brother Polynices, who had quarreled with him over the kingship of Thebes after their father's death. Aeschylus, in *Seven against Thebes;* Sophocles, in *Antigone* and *Oedipus at Colonus;* and Euripides, in *The Phoenician Women*, present other aspects of this story of rival brothers. Euripides here concerns himself not with the rights and wrongs of the dispute, but with the sufferings war brings to civilians. The play is best understood as a plea against inhumanity, especially in wartime. It is similar, in this respect, to Euripides' *The Trojan Women*, with the addition of a scene or two in favor of democracy, suggesting that the basic decencies of life have a better chance of being observed under popular than under autocratic government. And yet eloquent praises of peace (ll. 476–93) are put into the mouth of an antidemocratic person. Historically, this may reflect the war-weariness of the time; artistically, it shows that Euripides, like Shaw, lets all his parties have their say and say it well.

The action of the play is primarily ethical and political. Individual feelings take a minor role. Aethra, as her son points out (l. 292), has nothing to gain or lose by supporting the plea of the mothers of the seven warriors who fell in the attempt on the Theban throne. Theseus, at first reluctant to do anything for the pathetic Adrastus, overcomes his dislike of that ineffective person to the extent of defending his cause by force. It is evident that Euripides is holding Theseus up as an example of civic virtue, which he sees as flexible but not pliant —ready to change, for the better, under the influence of moral and religious arguments.

With Aethra and Theseus, models of principled moderation, Adrastus and Evadne provide an effective contrast. Both of them are capable of being carried away by feeling: Adrastus by guilt and shame, Evadne by love and grief. And both of them shock and repel better-balanced people: Adrastus irritates Theseus, Evadne horrifies her father and even the chorus, who interrupt their grief over their fallen sons to express amazement at Evadne's suicide (ll. 1072, 1076). Here Euripides' pity for humanity finds noble expression. He sees how war, and other extreme situations, bring out the essence of every individual: self-reproach in Adrastus, fanatical loyalty in Evadne, filial devotion in the sons of the Seven. And he also feels deeply the futility and cruelty of war, which keeps breeding new wars from old (ll. 1142–49), kills the noblest men, and lets Adrastus survive. With the morbid timidity of this king's actions and attitudes—for example, in lines 765–69—we may contrast the excellences he sees in his fallen companions (ll. 856–917). Yet even Adrastus redeems himself, somewhat, in the course of the action: his utterances become less hysterical and self-pitying, and he speaks out as an advocate of peace (ll. 949–54). He represents, in his fashion, the type of tragic hero who learns by suffering.

The intervention of Athene, at the end of the play, may seem pointless to modern readers. The passage possibly refers to an alliance of Athens with Argos, about 420 B.C. At any rate, Euripides here leaves the territory of philanthropic principle and talks hard political sense. Or perhaps he is suggesting that one is not much use without the other.

Lines 176–83 present some difficulty. It is likely that the poet is here defending himself against charges that he broke the decorum of tragedy by presenting paupers and slaves as serious personages. In lines 180–83, he is perhaps implying that sad scenes in a man's plays do not mean that he leads a sad life. The passage as a whole has little to do with what Adrastus is saying. Perhaps it was interpolated from another play, or lines linking it with Adrastus' main point have been lost. The opening of Theseus' answer (ll. 195–200) does not refer directly to anything Adrastus has said. It may be aimed at pessimistic implications of lines 176–79, which present life as perpetual conflict between wealth and poverty. These implications were perhaps more clearly worked out in the correct text. Whatever Adrastus said, Theseus thought he was questioning the motives or the very existence of the gods, on the ground that human life has more bad than good in it.

Lines 1026–30 are obscure in the original. Evadne seems to be inveighing against marriage, perhaps to fortify her resolve to die with the man she loves; but her picture of a happy home life belies her embittered intent. Either Euripides is being very subtle here or the text is corrupt.

The translation follows Gilbert Murray's text as edited by T. Nicklin (Oxford, 1936). At line 763 there is a lacuna, which I have ventured to fill with a question from Adrastus, as Nicklin suggests. But lines 844–45 of the Oxford text appear as lines 858–59 in this translation. If Theseus said (as he does in the text) "I saw the deeds . . . by which they hoped to take the city," it would mean that he had witnessed the attack of the Seven against Thebes. This is un-likely, and since the words would come much more properly from Adrastus at this point, I have transferred them to him. For similar reasons, line 162, spoken by Adrastus in the Oxford text, has been transferred to Theseus, as Valckenaer recommends.

THE SUPPLIANT WOMEN

CHARACTERS

Aethra, mother of Theseus

Theseus, king of Athens

Adrastus, king of Argos, and leader of the Theban adventure

A Herald from Thebes

A Messenger from Thebes

Evadne, widow of Capaneus, who fell in the Theban adventure

Iphis, her father

Athene

Chorus: Mothers of the Seven against Thebes

A group of sons of the fallen fighters

THE SUPPLIANT WOMEN

SCENE: *The temple of Demeter, at Eleusis, near Athens.*

Aethra

Demeter, enshrined in this land Eleusis,
And you who tend the goddess' temple,
Bless me and bless Theseus my son
And the city of Athens, and Pittheus' land,
Where in prosperous halls my father reared me, 5
Aethra, and wed me to Pandion's son
Aegeus, as Loxias' oracle bade him.

So I pray as I look upon these women
Burdened with years, who left their homes in Argos
To fall with suppliant branches at my feet 10
In dreadful loss: their seven noble sons
Are dead at Cadmus' gates, and they are childless.
Adrastus, lord of Argos, led the men
To claim for his son-in-law, exiled Polynices,
A share of Oedipus' inheritance. 15
They perished in the struggle, and their mothers
Desire to bury them; but those in power
Spurn what the gods hold lawful and refuse
Even to grant removal of the bodies.
The burden of these women's need for me 20
Adrastus also bears: look where he lies,
With tearful face mourning the grievous doom
That met the army he despatched from home.
Through me he seeks a champion in my son
Who shall prevail by words or force of arms 25
To take the dead and give them burial.
Only this he asks of my child and Athens.

My visit was for sacrifice
That the land be fruitful; I left my house

For this sanctuary, where soonest   30
The corn-ear bristles above the ground.
And still I stay by the holy hearth
Wearing a bondless bond of leaves,
In pity for these gray, childless mothers   35
And reverence for their sacred wreaths.
I have sent a herald to town, to summon
Theseus, that either he drive from the land
These people and the distress they bring,
Or free them from their suppliant needs—
A pious action for the gods.   40
It is proper for women, if they are wise,
Always to get things done by men.

Chorus

I appeal to you
From aged mouth:
Old, I fall at your knee.
Free my children—   45
Left by lawless men
To body-slackening death,
Food for mountain beasts!
See the piteous
Tears at my eyelids
And wrinkled tearings of hands   50
At hoary flesh
Because I could not lay out
My dead sons in my house
Or see their tombs of earth!

Gracious lady, you too have borne a son,
In blessing of the bed   55
For your husband: now to me
Grant a part of your loving-kindness,
In recompense for grievous pain

From the death of those I bore:
Prevail, we beg, upon your son   60
That he go to Ismenus and bring to my hands
The bodies of youthful dead that long for the tomb.

Not for holy rites but in need I came
To fall and pray at the goddesses'
Fire-receiving altars;
Justice is ours, and you have power—   65
For you are happy in your child—
To take away my trouble.
My plight is pitiful: I beseech
Your son to bring to these poor hands
The corpse, my son's sad limbs, for my embrace.   70

(*The temple attendants begin to chant.*)

And now the strife of wailing, wailing!
Cry against cry, clashing of priestesses' hands!
Let blows resound together!
Moan in the strain
Of the dance that Hades loves!   75
Bloody the white fingernail
Along the cheek, and stain the skin!
To mourn the dead
Brings honor to those who live.

Insatiable delight of wailing,
Abounding in labor, carries me away
As from a towering rock   80
Cool water flows
Unceasing ever: I wail,
For to bear the death of children brings
A labor of lament to women.   85
Would that in death
I might forget these griefs!

(*Enter Theseus, attended.*)

Theseus

> What were those wails I heard, and breast-beating,
> And dirges for the dead? Here, from the temple,
> The echoes came. Alarm takes hold of me:
> My mother has been long away from home;   90
> I come to find her; has she met with trouble?
>
> Aha! What's there? I see strange things to talk of!
> My aged mother sitting by the altar,
> And foreign women with her, all awry
> In shapes of woe: from age-dimmed eyes they shed   95
> Piteous tears to earth; their hair is shorn,
> The robes they wear are not for festivals.
> Mother, what does this mean? Yours to reveal,
> And mine to listen. I expect some ill.

Aethra

> These women, child, are mothers of the sons—   100
> Seven commanders—who died at Cadmus' gates;
> And now with suppliant boughs they watch and wait,
> Circled around me, as you see, my son.

Theseus

> And that one, groaning bitterly at the door?

Aethra

> They say he is Adrastus, lord of Argos.   105

Theseus

> And the boys beside him? Children of the women?

Aethra

> No, they are sons of the warriors who fell.

Theseus

> Why do they stretch out suppliant hands to us?

Aethra

  I know; but let them have the word, my son.

Theseus

  I call on you, hidden beneath your cloak!   110
  Leave off your wailing, bare your head and speak:
  Nothing goes far that does not pass the tongue.

Adrastus

  O glorious victor king
  Of the land of the men of Athens,
  Theseus: I come as suppliant
  To you and to your city.

Theseus

  What do you seek, and what is your need?   115

Adrastus

  You know of my ruinous campaign.

Theseus

  Your passage through Greece was hardly silent.

Adrastus

  In it I lost the chiefs of Argos.

Theseus

  Such are the doings of wretched war.

Adrastus

  I went to the city to find the dead.   120

Theseus

  For burial, by the laws of war?

Adrastus

  And now the slayers will not let me.

Theseus

  What are their grounds? Your wish is sacred.

Adrastus

  They have no grounds. They are bad winners.

Theseus

  So you come to me for advice—or what?   125

Adrastus

  I want you to bring back Argos' sons.

Theseus

  And where stands Argos? Are her boasts vain?

Adrastus

  Defeated, finished. We come to you.

Theseus

  By your design or that of all the city?

Adrastus

  We, the Danaids, beg you to bury our dead.   130

Theseus

  Why did you go with seven bands to Thebes?

Adrastus

  To please the men who married my two daughters.

Theseus

  To which of the Argives did you give your children?

Adrastus

  The bond I formed was not among my kind.

Theseus

  To strangers, then, you wedded Argive girls?   135

Adrastus

Yes: Tydeus, and Polynices, of Theban stock.

Theseus

How did you come to want them for your kin?

Adrastus

Puzzling riddles of Phoebus lured me on.

Theseus

What words of Apollo meant marriage for the maidens?

Adrastus

That I give my daughters to a boar and a lion.   140

Theseus

And how did you unravel the god's pronouncement?

Adrastus

The pair of exiles came to my door at night—

Theseus

What pair? You speak of two at once: explain.

Adrastus

Tydeus and Polynices—and fought each other.

Theseus

They were the beasts? You gave your girls to them?   145

Adrastus

Yes, they looked like two wild creatures fighting.

Theseus

Why had they left the borders of their countries?

Adrastus

Tydeus in guilt of shedding kindred blood.

Theseus

And what brought Oedipus' son away from Thebes?

Adrastus

A father's curse: that he should kill his brother.   150

Theseus

Then voluntary flight was wise of him.

Adrastus

True; but those remaining wronged the absent.

Theseus

You mean his brother robbed him of his goods?

Adrastus

That is the case I went to judge; and lost.

Theseus

You asked the seers, and watched their victims burn?   155

Adrastus

Ah! You pursue me to my weakest point.

Theseus

The gods, it seems, did not approve your mission.

Adrastus

It also flouted Amphiaraus' will.

Theseus

So lightly you ignored divinity?

Adrastus

Unruliness of youthful men confused me.   160

Theseus

You followed strength of heart, not strength of mind—
A course that ruins many generals.

Adrastus

O Lord of Athens! Crown of power in Hellas!
I am ashamed—a gray-haired man who once
Was king, and fortunate—that now I fall
To earth and clasp your knee; and yet I must   165
Submit to my disaster. Save my dead!
Have pity on my woes, and on these mothers
Of fallen sons! Struck childless in old age   170
With feeble limbs they come to a strange land—
Not to attend Demeter's mysteries,
But seeking burial of the dead whose hands,
In manly duty, should have buried *them*.   175
The sight of poverty is wise for wealth;
The poor should gaze with envy on the rich,
To learn the love of goods; untroubled men
Are well advised to look at wretchedness.
The poet bringing songs into the world   180
Should work in joy. If this is not his mood,
He cannot—being inwardly distressed—
Give pleasure outwardly. That stands to reason.
You may well ask: "Why pass by Pelops' land,
And seek to lay this task of yours on Athens?"   185
In fairness, I would make this answer. Sparta
Is fierce; her ways are artful; and the others
Are small and weak. Yours is the only city
With strength enough to undertake the task:
She sees what misery is and has for leader,   190
In you, a good and youthful shepherd; ruin
Has come to many states for lack of such command.

Chorus

Theseus! I join my prayer to his:
Pity my wretchedness.

Theseus

I have heard such arguments before, from others,   195
And fought them hard. It has been said that life
Holds more of worse conditions than of better;
But I oppose that doctrine. I believe
The good outweighs the bad in human life.
If it did not, the light would not be ours.   200
I praise the god who set our life in order,
Lifting it out of savagery and confusion.
First he put wits in us, and then gave language,
Envoy of words, to understand the voice;
And fruits of earth to eat, and for this food   205
Watery drops from heaven, to quench our thirst
And nourish the yield of the land; providing also
The fortress winter, against the sun-god's fire,
And commerce over sea, that by exchange
A country may obtain the goods it lacks.   210
Things without mark, not clearly visible,
Are brought to light by seers who study fire,
The folds of entrails, and the flight of birds.
Now, if all this is not enough for us—
So well equipped for living, by God's gift—   215
Are we not pettish? But intelligence
Wants more than heavenly power; our minds grow proud,
Until we think we are wiser than the gods.
That is the brand of folly you have shown.
First, bowing to Phoebus' words, like one who thinks   220
The gods exist, you gave your girls to strangers:
A mating of fair with foul, to hurt your house!
Wrongdoers' bodies should not be joined to the just;
A wise man will ally his family
With well-regarded people. Sickness spreads: 225
A man may do no wrong; yet, if he suffers
From the same ill as one marked out for ruin,
God fells them both at once.

Then, when you took
All Argos with you on that expedition,
The seers spoke omens but you slighted them,   230
Flouted the gods, and laid your city low.
You were led astray by glory-loving youngsters,
Promoters of unjust wars, who spoil the townsmen.
One of them wants to be a general;
Another to seize power and riot in it;   235
A third is set on gain. They never think
What harm this brings for the majority.
The classes of citizens are three. The rich
Are useless, always lusting after more.
Those who have not, and live in want, are a menace,   240
Ridden with envy and fooled by demagogues;
Their malice stings the owners. Of the three,
The middle part saves cities: it guards the order   245
A community establishes.

And so
I am to be your ally? What fine words
Will make my citizens favor that? Farewell!
You planned your actions poorly. Take what comes:
Wrestle with fate alone, and let me be.

Chorus

He blundered. That is natural in the young,   250
And should be pardoned in him. We have come
To you, my lord, as healer of these ills,

Adrastus

In choosing you, my lord, I did not think
That you would sit in judgment on my woes,
Or estimate and punish any act   255
I may have lacked the skill to carry out;
I only wanted help. If you refuse,
I have no choice; I must obey.

Now, aged dames, go forth. Lay on that spot
The verdant twigs, and turn the leaves face down,
Calling to witness heaven and earth and sun   260
And Queen Demeter, bearer of the torch,
That prayers to the gods availed us nothing.

Chorus

O King, you are of Pelops' line, and we are from his country:
The same ancestral blood is ours. How can it be
That *you* forsake this cause, and drive out of your land   265
Old women who have gained nothing that is owed them?
We pray you not to do this. Beasts have rocks for refuge;
Slaves, the altars of the gods; city huddles with city
When storms come. Nothing mortal prospers to the end.   270

—Woman of sorrows! Leave Persephone's sacred ground;
Go up to him and put your hands about his knees;
Beg him to bring my sons' dead bodies—Oh, the grief!
The young men whom I lost beneath Cadmean walls.

—Alas! these poor old hands: take them, guide them, support   275
them.

—Friend! Honor and glory of Hellas! I touch your beard;
Here at your knees I fall and seek your hand in my woe.

—If you would shelter a wanderer, pity me—   280
Suppliant for my children, piteously lamenting.

—Child! I appeal to you: do not leave boys your age
Unburied in Cadmus' land, to gladden the wild beasts!

—I fall and clasp your knees: see the tears at my eyelids!
I beg you, bring to fulfilment the burial of my children!   285

Theseus

Mother: you hold your fine-spun cloak to your eyes.
Why do you weep? Is it because you hear

The lamentations uttered by these women?
Somehow, they pierce me too. Raise your white head:
No more tears, at Demeter's sacred hearth!   290

Aethra

   Alas!

Theseus

      Their troubles should not make you moan.

Aethra

   Poor women!

Theseus

          You do not belong to them.

Aethra

   Child! May I speak, for the city's good and yours?

Theseus

   Many wise things are said even by women.

Aethra

   I shrink from showing what I have in mind.   295

Theseus

   It is shameful to hold back words that might help your kin.

Aethra

   I would not now be still, and afterward
Blame myself for a silence wrongly kept;
Or fear that women's well-meant words are wasted,
And in that dread let my good will be lost.   300
My child: I bid you: first, look to the gods;
For if you slight them you will fall. Intentions
Good in themselves are wrecked by that one fault.
If you were asked to launch an enterprise
That would not right a wrong, then certainly   305

I would be silent. But you must be told
How greatly it would honor you (so much
That I am not afraid to urge it, child!)
If cruel men, who would deny the dead
The rights of burial and their funerals,
Were forced to grant this, by your hand, and stopped   310
From violating what all Greece holds lawful.
The power that keeps cities of men together
Is noble preservation of the laws.
It will be said that, lacking manly strength,
You stood aside in fear and lost a chance   315
To win a crown of glory for the city.
They will say you hunted boars, a mean pursuit,
And proved a coward at the call of action,
The time for spear and helmet. Child of mine,
This must not be! Remember your descent!   320
Do you see your country's Gorgon stare when taunted
With lack of resolution? Athens thrives
On strenuous action; but the states that work
In stealth and darkness wear a somber look   325
To match their caution. Child, will you not help
The dead, and these poor women in their need?
Your setting forth is just; I do not dread it.
The sons of Cadmus now have won the throw,
But soon the dice will fall another way.   330
I hold this certain. God reverses all.

Chorus

O best-loved lady! Nobly have you spoken,
For him and me, giving a double joy.

Theseus

Mother, what I have said about this man
I still consider right. I spoke my mind   335
On the designs that led him to his ruin.
But I also see the truth of what you tell me:

That it is not in keeping with my ways
To run from risk. By many noble deeds
I have made myself a byword to the Greeks: 340
They count on me to punish wickedness.
I am unable to refuse a task.
What then will hostile persons say of me
If you, my parent, you who fear for me,
Must urge me first to undertake this labor?   345
Forward, then; I shall go and free the dead.
Persuasion first: if that does not succeed,
Then force of arms will gain my end. The gods
Will not be jealous. I desire the city
With all its voices to approve this plan.
It will approve because I want it to: 350
But if I state my reasons, I shall have
More favor from the people, whom I made
Sole rulers when I set their city free
And gave them equal votes. So I shall take
Adrastus to support my argument
And go to all the citizens assembled,   355
Convince them that this must be done, pick out
A group of young Athenians, and return.
Then, resting on my weapons, I shall send
To ask the bodies of the dead from Creon.
Matrons: take off my mother's ritual garlands.
I must conduct her to the house of Aegeus,   360
Clasping her loving hand. I think it wrong
That a child should not return his parents' care.
Noblest of gifts! by granting it, he earns
From his own children what he gives his elders.

Chorus

Argos, my fatherland, pasture of horses: 365
You heard him speak, you heard from the king
Words that respect the gods,
Words that mean greatness for Greece and Argos.

May he go to the end of my woes, and beyond;
May he bear the mother's murdered idol   370
Away, and then make friendship
Firm with the land of Inachus.

A work of piety brings honor and glory to cities
And earns thanks that last forever.
What dare I hope from the city? Will it truly gain   375
A pledge of friendship, and graves for my sons?

City of Pallas! A mother begs you to prevent
The desecration of human law.
You revere right, despise crime, and are ready
Always to help ill-fated men.   380

Theseus (to an Athenian herald)
  The skill you have as bearer of proclamations
  Has given constant service to me and the city.
  Now you must cross the streams Asopus and Ismenus
  And tell the haughty ruler of the Cadmeans this:
"Theseus asks you, by your grace, to bury the dead. His country   385
  Neighbors yours, and he believes the request is worth the
     granting.
  Do this and you will have all of Erechtheus' folk for friends."
  If they consent, commend them and hasten back.
  If they refuse, deliver a second message:
"Welcome my band of revelers, men who carry shields!"   390
  A ready task-force waits, under review,
  Here and now at the sacred Fount of the Dance.
  The city, when it saw I willed this effort,
  Was ready to accept it, even glad.

  But who comes here, to interrupt my words?   395
  I cannot tell for sure; he seems to be
  A Theban herald. Stay a while. His coming
  Might change my plans, and you would be released.

(Enter a Herald from Thebes.)

Herald

What man is master in this land? To whom
Must I give the word I bring from Creon, ruler   400
In Cadmus' country since Eteocles
Fell at his brother Polynices' hand
Beside the seven-mouthed gates?

Theseus

                    One moment, stranger.
Your start was wrong, seeking a master here.
This city is free, and ruled by no one man.   405
The people reign, in annual succession.
They do not yield the power to the rich;
The poor man has an equal share in it.

Herald

That one point gives the better of the game
To me. The town I come from is controlled   410
By one man, not a mob. And there is no one
To puff it up with words, for private gain,
Swaying it this way, that way. Such a man
First flatters it with wealth of favors; then
He does it harm, but covers up his blunders   415
By blaming other men, and goes scot-free.
The people is no right judge of arguments;
Then how can it give right guidance to a city?
A poor man, working hard, could not attend   420
To public matters, even if ignorance
Were not his birthright. When a wretch, a nothing,
Obtains respect and power from the people
By talk, his betters sicken at the sight.   425

Theseus

What bombast from a herald! Waster of words,
If it is argument you want—and you yourself

Have set the contest going—listen. Nothing
Is worse for a city than an absolute ruler.
In earliest days, before the laws are common, 430
One man has power and makes the law his own:
Equality is not yet. With written laws,
People of small resources and the rich
Both have the same recourse to justice. Now
A man of means, if badly spoken of, 435
Will have no better standing than the weak;
And if the little man is right, he wins
Against the great. This is the call of freedom:
"What man has good advice to give the city,
And wishes to make it known?" He who responds 440
Gains glory; the reluctant hold their peace.
For the city, what can be more fair than that?
Again, when the people is master in the land,
It welcomes youthful townsmen as its subjects;
But when one man is king, he finds this hateful,
And if he thinks that any of the nobles 445
Are wise, he fears for his despotic power
And kills them. How can a city become strong
If someone takes away, cuts off new ventures
Like ears of corn in a spring field? What use
To build a fortune, if your work promotes 450
The despot's welfare, not your family's?
Why bring up girls as gentlewomen, fit
For marriage, if tyrants may take them for their joy—
A grief to parents? I would rather die
Than see my children forced to such a union. 455
    These are the darts I shoot at what you say.
What have you come to ask of this, our country?
You talk too much; you would regret your visit
Had not a city sent you. Messengers
Should state their mission promptly, then return. 460
I hope that henceforth, to my city, Creon
Sends a less wordy messenger than you.

Chorus

When fortune aids the wicked, how they revel!
They act as if their luck would last forever.

Herald

Now I shall speak. On what has been debated,   465
You may hold your views; I the opposite.
    I and the whole Cadmean people say
Adrastus must not pass into this land.
If he has entered it, you must strip off
His sacred ritual wreaths and drive him out   470
Before the sun-god's flame is down. His dead
Must not be removed by force; the Argives' city
Is no concern of yours. Do what I say
And you will steer your city's course in calm.
If you refuse, there will be much rough water
For us, for you, and for our allies: war.   475
Think now: do not let anger at my words
Goad you to puffed-up answers. You are free;
That does not make you powerful. Hope has driven
Many cities against each other; she stirs
An overreaching heart; she is not to be trusted.   480
When the people vote on war, nobody reckons
On his own death; it is too soon; he thinks
Some other man will meet that wretched fate.
But if death faced him when he cast his vote,
Hellas would never perish from battle-madness.   485
And yet we men all know which of two words
Is better, and can weigh the good and bad
They bring: how much better is peace than war!
First and foremost, the Muses love her best;
And the goddess of vengeance hates her. She delights   490
In healthy children, and she glories in wealth.
But evilly we throw all this away
To start our wars and make the losers slaves—
Man binding man and city chaining city.

And you would help our enemies in death,
Taking away for burial men who fell   495
By their own pride? Do you not think it right
That thunderbolts made smoke of Capaneus,
The one who thrust the ladders at the gates
And swore to sack the city whether God
Willed it or not? The bird-interpreter,
Was he not swallowed by a gulf that opened   500
Around his four-horse chariot? There they lie,
The other squadron-leaders, by the gates;
Rocks have crushed the framework of their bones.
Now boast a greater mind than Zeus, or grant
That the bad are justly punished by the gods.   505
Wise men should cherish children first, then parents,
Then fatherland—and that they ought to strengthen,
Not enervate. A bold leader or sailor
Brings peril; the man who knows when not to act
Is wise. To my mind, bravery is forethought.   510

Chorus

Zeus the punisher was enough. No need
For you to gloat like this over their doom.

Adrastus

You miserable wretch—

Theseus

                    Silence, Adrastus!
Restrain yourself. Do not give precedence
To your words over mine. This challenge comes   515
To me, not you; and I must answer it.

                                   (*To the herald.*)

I have not heard that Creon is my master,
Or even more powerful than I. How then
Can he compel Athens to do his bidding?
If we serve him, the world runs backward! I   520

Did not begin this war: I was not with them
When they went to Thebes; I only think it just
To bury their dead. I mean no harm to the city,
No man-destroying struggles: I uphold   525
The law of all the Greeks. Is that unfair?
Yes, certainly the Argives did you wrong,
But they are dead. You fought them off with honor,
To their disgrace; and now the case is closed.   530
Come! Let the dead be covered by the ground,
And let each part regain the element
From which it came to light: the spirit, air;
The body, earth. The flesh is only ours
To dwell in while life lasts; and afterward   535
The giver of its strength must take it back.
Do you think to hurt Argos by leaving her dead unburied?
You miss your mark. All Hellas is concerned
When anyone tries to strip the dead of their due
And keep them from the tomb. If that were law,   540
Brave men would turn cowards. And yet you come
To threaten me with frightful words. Do you dread
The corpses? If they are hidden in earth, what then?
Will they overthrow your country from the grave,
Or beget children in the womb of earth   545
Who will avenge them some day? Fears like these
Are base and vain, a waste of breath to speak.
Fools! Be instructed in the ills of man.
Struggles make up our life. Good fortune comes   550
Swiftly to some, to some hereafter; others
Enjoy it now. Its god luxuriates.
Not only is he honored by the hapless
In hope of better days, but lucky ones
Exalt him too, fearing to lose the wind.
Aware of this, you should not take it hard   555
When moderately wronged, or do a wrong
So great that it will hurt your city. Therefore
You ought to grant the bodies of the fallen

To us, who wish to do them reverence.
If you choose otherwise, my course is clear: 560
I shall compel their burial. Never the Greeks
Shall have this news to tell: that ancient law,
Established by the gods, appealed to me
And Pandion's city, only to be shattered.

Chorus

Courage! Keep alive the light of justice,
And much that men say in blame will pass you by. 565

Herald

May I make a speech that is short and plain?

Theseus

Say what you like: you are no mute.

Herald

You will never take Argos' sons from my country.

Theseus

Now hear me, if you will, in turn.

Herald

I listen; I must grant your due. 570

Theseus

I shall bury the dead away from Thebes.

Herald

First you must risk a clash of shields.

Theseus

I have come through many other trials.

Herald

Did your father make you a match for all?

Theseus

Offenders, yes; I do not crush virtue. 575

Herald

You and your city have busy habits.

Theseus

Endeavor brings prosperity.

Herald

Go, and be caught by a Sown Man's spear!

Theseus

What martial fury can come from a dragon?

Herald

Feel it and know it. You are still young. 580

Theseus

You cannot rouse my mind to wrath
By boasting. Take the foolish words
You brought, and leave the country. Talk
Will gain us nothing.

(*The Theban Herald goes out.*)

         Forward, every man 585
Who fights on foot or from a chariot!
Let cheek-pieces rattle, flecking the horses' mouths
With foam as they gallop toward the Theban land!
I march on Cadmus' seven gates; I bear
Sharp iron in my hand and act as herald 590
In my behalf. Adrastus, I command you,
Stay here; do not attach your fate to me.
I shall lead the army, guided by my god,
As a new campaigner with a new intent.
Only one thing I need: to have with me
The gods who honor justice. That support 595

Gives victory. Human excellence means nothing
Unless it works with the consent of God.

(Exeunt Theseus and attendants; Aethra.)

Chorus

Pitiful mothers of lost commanders!
Yellow fear sits on my heart.

—What new word is this you bring?   600

—How will the mission of Pallas stand the test?

—By fighting, did you say, or exchange of words?

—I pray that good will come of it!
But what if it ends in slayings by Ares,
Battles, din of beaten breasts throughout the city?   605
Then, alas! What could I find to say,
I, who caused it all?

—The man who glories in his luck
May be overthrown by destiny;
In that hope I rest secure.

—Then you believe in gods who stand for justice.   610

—Of course; what other beings make things happen?

—I see much else in the way they treat us.

—That is because you are crushed by fear
From the past. But justice has called for justice, blood for blood;
The gods, who hold in their hands the end of all,
Now give men rest from pain.   615

—How might we leave the sacred fount of the goddess
And reach the plains with the beautiful towers?

—If one of the gods would give you wings,   620

—On the way to the two-rivered city.

—You would know, then you would know how our friends are
faring.

—What destiny, what turn of fate, I wonder,
Is waiting for this country's mighty lord?   625

—Again we call on gods invoked already:
Here is the foremost hope of the frightened.

—O Zeus, who fathered a child for the heifer
Of Inachus, mother of old,
Favor this my city and help its cause.   630
Your image, the city's mainstay, has been outraged;
And I would make it ready for the pyre.

(*Enter a Messenger from Thebes.*)

Messenger

Women, I bring much news that you will welcome.
I have come through to safety after capture   635
In the battle which the seven companies
Of fallen masters fought by Dirce's stream.
I am here to tell of Theseus' victory.
To spare you long inquiry: I was a servant
Of Capaneus, whom Zeus's flaming bolt   640
Riddled to ashes.

Chorus

Oh, with joy we greet
Your news of coming home, and hear the word
You bring of Theseus! If Athens' army too
Is safe, then all you have to tell is welcome.

Messenger

Safe; and it did what should have been achieved
By Adrastus with the Argives whom he marched   645
From Inachus against the Cadmean city.

Chorus

How did the son of Aegeus and his comrades
Gain victory? Tell us now. You saw it happen;
You can give joy to those who were not there.

Messenger

A brilliant shaft of sunlight, straight and clear,   650
Lit up the field as I stood at Electra gate,
Where a tower gave a sweeping view. I saw
Three forces marshalled. Infantry with armor
Extended toward high ground: the Ismenian hill,   655
I heard it called. The famous son of Aegeus,
With men from old Cecropia held the right;
The left wing, spear-armed Coast men, took positions
Beside the spring of Ares. Cavalry massed   660
At each wing's end, in equal groups; and chariots
Stood at the foot of Amphion's sacred mound.   665
Cadmus' men, posted before the walls, had put
The bodies, cause of conflict, at their rear.
Horsemen faced horsemen; chariots stood ready,
Equipped to battle four-horse chariots.
Then Theseus' herald spoke these words to all:
Silence, my men; silence, Cadmean troops.
Hear me: we come to take the dead. We wish   670
To bury them, and so uphold the law
Of all the Greeks. It is not our desire
To shed more blood." Creon gave no command
To answer this, but stood in silence, ready.
Then the charioteers began the combat.   675
Driving their chariots toward and past each other,
They set their fighters down, in line of battle.
While these crossed swords, the drivers turned their horses
Back to support their men. When Phorbas, captain   680
Of Athens' horsemen, and the overseers
Of Theban cavalry saw the chariots clustered,
They threw their forces into the tide of war.

As witness, not from hearsay—I was close
To the battleground of chariots and riders—   685
I know the many horrors there, but not
Where to begin. With the dust that rose toward heaven?
How thick it was! Or men tossed up and down,
Caught in the horses' reins? Or streams of blood   690
From men who fell, or were flung head first to earth
When cars were shattered, leaving life beside
Wreckage of chariots? When Creon saw
Our mounted forces winning, he took his shield   695
And moved to keep his allies from despair.
Then all the middle of the field was spattered
As men slew and were slain; and the word passed,   700
Shouted aloud among them: "Strike! Thrust back
The spear at Erechtheus' sons!" But Theseus' fortunes
Were not to fall by terror. Snatching up
His shining arms, he charged at once. Fiercely
The host that grew to men from dragon's teeth
Opposed us, pushing our left wing back; but theirs   705
Lost to our right and fled. The scales of war
Stood even. Then our general earned praise;
Not seeking only to follow up advantage,
He hurried to his forces' breaking-point,
Shouting so loud that he made the earth resound: 710
"Hold, lads, against these dragon men's stiff spears,
Or else farewell to Athens!" That stirred courage
Throughout the Cranaid army. Then he seized
His Epidaurian weapon, a ghastly club,
And swung it right and left, dealing his blows   715
On heads and necks together; the wooden blade
Mowed off and snapped their helmets; turning to flee,
They could hardly move their feet. I shrieked and danced
And clapped my hands. The Thebans made for the gates.   720
Then there were cries and groans throughout the city
From young and old; frightened, they thronged the temples.
Now Theseus might have gone inside the walls;

But he held back, declaring that his purpose
Was not to sack the town but claim the dead. 725
   That is the kind of general to elect:
One who puts forth his strength in time of trouble,
And hates the greedy mob that tries to climb
To the top of the ladder even when times are good,
And wrecks the happiness it might enjoy. 730

Chorus

Now, having seen this day, surpassing hope,
I believe in gods. The lesser share of evil
Seems to be mine now; Thebes has paid the price.

Adrastus

Zeus! Who dares call us hapless mortals wise?
You dangle us; whatever you want, we do. 735
Argos, we thought, was irresistible:
We were so many, young, and strong of arm!
Eteocles would have come to terms; his claims
Were fair; but we refused, and lost. 740
The winner then, malignant folk of Cadmus,
Ran riot like a pauper newly rich;
But now their rioting brings them down, in turn.
O you who try to shoot beyond the mark!
O witless mortals! Richly you deserve 745
Your many woes; you listen not to friends,
But to your interests. Cities! You might use
Reason to end your troubles; but with blood,
Not words, you ruin your affairs.—Enough! 750

                        (*To the messenger.*)

   I would like to know how you reached safety;
Then I will ask my other questions.

Messenger

When the city shook in turmoil of war,
I went through the gates where the troops came in.

Adrastus

Do you bring the dead for whom they fought?

Messenger

Yes, the heads of the seven great houses.   755

Adrastus

But the mass of the fallen—where are they?

Messenger

Buried near Cithaeron's folds.

Adrastus

This side, or that? By whom were they buried?

Messenger

At Eleutherae's shady ridge. By Theseus.

Adrastus

Those he did not bury—where have you left them?   760

Messenger

Close by. Speed makes all roads short.

Adrastus

Did it pain the servants to bring them out of the carnage?

Messenger

No one who was a slave had charge of that.

Adrastus

Did Theseus welcome the task?

Messenger

                                    You would have said so
If you had seen his loving salute to the dead.

Adrastus

And did he wash the victims' stains himself?   765

Messenger

He even spread the couches and covered the bodies.

Adrastus

That was a dreadful burden, bringing shame.

Messenger

How can our common ills be shameful to us?

Adrastus

Oh, how much rather had I died with them!

Messenger

Your laments are vain, and make these women weep.   770

Adrastus

Yes. It was they who taught me. Now I cease.
Let me lift up my hand when I meet the dead,
And speak, in long and tearful chants of Hades,
To friends by whom I am left to mourn alone.
If you lose money you can get it back, but no one   775
Recovers this expense: a human life.

                              (*The Messenger goes out.*)

Chorus

Part well, part ill—this turn of fate.
For city and soldiers who went to war,   780
Glory and honor redoubled;
For me, to look upon my children's bodies—
A bitter, lovely sight, if ever I see it
And the day despaired of,
Greatest pain of all.   785
Would that old Time, father of days,
Had left me unwed all my life.
What need had I of children?
Once, I thought, I could not bear the sorrow   790

Of being barred from wedlock. Now—
In loss of dearest children—
Its evil is plain to see.

(Attendants enter, bearing the corpses
of the fallen chiefs.)

The woeful sight has come: my fallen children's bodies!   795
Oh, to join them in death and go down to Hades together!

Adrastus

Mothers! Wail for the dead who lie on the ground!
Wail in answer when you hear my moans!   800

Chorus

Children! I bid you now in death
A bitter farewell for loving mothers.

Adrastus

O grief, O grief!

Chorus

     For my own woes I cry.   805

Adrastus

We have borne

Chorus

    the most tormenting evils.

Adrastus

O Argive city! Do your folk not see my downfall?

Chorus

They see me too in my wretched state, barren of children.   810

Adrastus

Bring on the bloodstained bodies of the doomed—
Champions in war, laid low by lesser men.

Chorus

    Give me my children to take in my arms;   815
    My hands are ready for that embrace.

Adrastus

    You have and hold

Chorus

                burden enough of woes.

Adrastus

    Alas!

Chorus

      No word for the parents?

Adrastus

    Hear me.

Chorus

        You groan with your pain and mine.   820

Adrastus

    I wish the Theban columns had struck me down in the dust.

Chorus

    Would that my body had never been yoked to a husband's bed.

Adrastus

    O wretched mothers of children!   825
    Behold, a sea of troubles.

Chorus

    Our nails cut furrows down our cheeks;
    We have poured dust over our heads.

Adrastus

    Oh, Oh, alas, alas!
    Swallow me, earth!

Hurricane, tear me apart!   830
Blaze of Zeus's fire, swoop down upon me!

Chorus

Bitter the wedding you saw,
Bitter the word of Phoebus;
A Fury, bringer of grief,
Has abandoned Oedipus' house and come to yours.   835

(Enter Theseus and Athenian soldiers.)

Theseus

(To an Argive captain.)

During your long lament before the army
I would have asked you this, but I refrained
From speaking then, and now I let it pass;   840
Here is Adrastus.

(To Adrastus.)

These are men whose spirit
Has brought them fame. What is their lineage?
Speak, from your greater knowledge, to the young
Among our citizens; you have understanding.   845
One thing I ask not, or you'd laugh at me;
Beside whom every warrior stood in battle,
Or from what foe he took a spear-wound. Vain
To tell or hear such tales—as if a man   850
In the thick of combat, with a storm of spears
Before his eyes, ever brought back sure news
On who was hero, I can neither ask
Ouch questions nor believe those who make bold
To answer them. When you stand against the foe,   855
It is hard enough to see what must be seen.

Adrastus

Hear, then. By granting me the privilege
Of praising friends, you meet my own desire
To speak of them with justice and with truth.

I saw the deeds—bolder than words can tell—
By which they hoped to take the city. Look:
The handsome one is Capaneus. Through him   860
The lightning went. A man of means, he never
Flaunted his wealth but kept an attitude
No prouder than a poor man's. He avoided
People who live beyond their needs and load
Their tables to excess. He used to say
That good does not consist in belly-food,   865
And satisfaction comes from moderation.
He was true in friendship to present and absent friends;
Not many men are so. His character
Was never false; his ways were courteous;
His word, in house or city, was his bond.   870
Second I name Eteoclus. He practiced
Another kind of virtue. Lacking means,
This youth held many offices in Argos.
Often his friends would make him gifts of gold,   875
But he never took them into his house. He wanted
No slavish way of life, haltered by money.
He kept his hate for sinners, not the city;
A town is not to blame if a bad pilot
Makes men speak ill of it. Hippomedon,   880
Third of the heroes, showed his nature thus:
While yet a boy he had the strength of will
Not to take up the pleasures of the Muses
That soften life; he went to live in the country,
Giving himself hard tasks to do, rejoicing   885
In manly growth. He hunted, delighted in horses,
And stretched the bow with his hands, to make his body
Useful to the city. There lies the son
Of huntress Atalanta, Parthenopaeus,
Supreme in beauty. He was Arcadian,
But came to Inachus' banks and was reared in Argos. 890
After his upbringing there, he showed himself,

As resident foreigners should, not troublesome
Or spiteful to the city, or disputatious,
Which would have made him hard to tolerate   895
As citizen and guest. He joined the army
Like a born Argive, fought the country's wars,
Was glad when the city prospered, took it hard
If bad times came. Although he had many lovers,
And women flocked to him, still he was careful   900
To cause them no offense. In praise of Tydeus
I shall say much in little. He was ambitious,
Greatly gifted, and wise in deeds, not words.
From what I have told you, Theseus, you should not wonder
That these men dared to die before the towers.   910
To be well brought up develops self-respect:
Anyone who has practiced what is good
Is ashamed to turn out badly. Manliness
Is teachable. Even a child is taught
To say and hear what he does not understand;   915
Things understood are kept in mind till age.
So, in like manner, train your children well.

Chorus

O my child, to an evil fate I bred you!
I carried you in my womb
And felt the pangs of birth;   920
Now, alas! Hades holds my burden,
And I have none to cherish me in age,
Though I bore a child, to my sorrow.

Theseus

And what of Oicles' noble son? His praises   925
Are uttered by the gods, who bore him off
Alive, with his chariot, into the depths of earth.
I too, in all sincerity, might honor
Oedipus' son: I speak of Polynices.
After leaving Cadmus' town, he stayed with me   930

Till he chose Argos for his place of exile.
Now, do you know what I wish to do with the fallen?

Adrastus

This only I know—to obey your orders.

Theseus

Capaneus, struck by Zeus's fire—

Adrastus

You will bury apart, as a sacred corpse?   935

Theseus

Yes. One pyre for all the others.

Adrastus

Where will you set his single memorial?

Theseus

Beside this shrine I will build the tomb.

Adrastus

The slaves may look to that labor now.

Theseus

And I to the rest. Bearers, move on.   940

> (*The attendants take up the biers.*)

Adrastus

Sorrowful mothers! Draw near your children!

Theseus

Adrastus! That was not well said.

Adrastus

Why? Must the parents not touch their children?

Theseus

To see their state would be mortal pain.

Adrastus

Yes; corpse-wounds and blood are a bitter sight.   945

Theseus

Then why would you increase the women's woe?

Adrastus

I yield.

(To the women.)

You must be brave, and stay where you are.
Theseus is right. When we put them to the fire,
You will take home their bones. O wretched mortals,
Why do you slaughter each other with your spears?   950
Leave off those struggles; let your towns take shelter
In gentleness. Life is a short affair;
We should try to make it smooth, and free from strife.

Chorus

Blest no more with children, blest no more with sons,   955
I have no share in happiness
Among the boy-bearing women of Argos.
And Artemis, who watches over birth,
Would have no word for childless women.
Life is a time of woe;   960
I am like a wandering cloud
Sent hurtling by fierce winds.
Seven mothers, we gave birth to seven sons
Who gained the heights of fame in Argos;   965
But that has brought us suffering.
And now, without a son, without a child,
Most miserably I grow old,
Neither a living creature
Nor one of the dead, my fate
Somehow apart from both.   970

Tears are left to me; sad
Memorials of my son are in my house:

Locks of his hair, and wreaths for mine, in mourning,
Libations for the vanished dead, and songs   975
Unwelcome to golden-haired Apollo.
At every dawn I shall wake to weep
And drench the folds of my dress at the breast with tears.

Already I can see the vaults   980
Of the sacred tomb of Capaneus,
And Theseus' memorials to the dead, outside the temple.
And close at hand I see Evadne,
Famous wife of him who died by lightning,   985
Daughter of Iphis the king.
Why has she climbed that path
To stand on a lofty rock
That towers above this shrine?

                                        (*Enter Evadne.*)

Evadne

Over what blaze, what gleam did sun and moon   990
Drive their chariots through the air
Where the light-bringers ride,
On that dark day when Argos' city   995
Built towers of song and greetings
For my wedding and the bridegroom,
Bronze-armored Capaneus? Alas!
To you I come, wildly running from home!   1000
I shall enter the glow of the pyre and share your grave,
Making Hades my release
From the weary weight of life
And the pain of being.   1005
This is the sweetest death: to die with loved ones dying,
If God should so decree.

Chorus

You see the pyre; you stand above and near it;
It is a treasure-house of Zeus. There lies   1010
Your husband, victim of the lightning-flash.

Evadne

From here I see how I shall end.
May fortune guide the leap of my feet to glory.   1015
From this rock I will dive
Into the flames. My body will mingle
In fiery glow with my husband,   1020
His loved flesh close to mine.
So shall I come to Persephone's halls,
Resolved never to cheat your death by living
Upon this earth. Daylight, wedlock, farewell!   1025
Away with Argive marriages
Shown to be true by children!
Out of my sight,
Devoted man of the house, drawn to your noble wife
By steady winds of love!   1030

Chorus

Your father, aged Iphis, comes upon
Strange words, unheard-of, that will hurt to hear.

                                              (*Enter Iphis.*)

Iphis

O women of sorrows! To my sorrowful age
My family has brought a double grief.   1035
I have come to take my dead son home by ship—
Eteoclus, who fell to the Theban spear—
And to seek my daughter, wife of Capaneus,
Who sped from my house in longing to die with her husband.
In former days, she was watched at home; beset   1040
By present troubles, I dismissed the guards;
And she has gone. I think she must be here;
If you have seen her, tell me.

Evadne

                        Why ask them?   1045
I am here on a rock above his pyre, my father—
Lightly poised, like a bird, for a flight of doom.

Iphis

    My child, what wind has blown you here? What errand?
    Why did you slip from home and come to this land?

Evadne

    You would be angry if I told my plans;   1050
    I do not wish you to hear about them, Father.

Iphis

    What? Is it not right that your father should know?

Evadne

    You would not be an able judge of my intent.

Iphis

    For whom have you put on this finery?

Evadne

    My dress has glory in its meaning, Father.   1055

Iphis

    You are not like one in mourning for her husband.

Evadne

    No, I have made myself ready for something new.

Iphis

    And yet you appear beside a tomb and a pyre!

Evadne

    I come to celebrate a victory.

Iphis

    I beg you, tell me over whom you won it.   1060

Evadne

    Over all women on whom the sun looks down.

Iphis

    In Athena's skills, or in the ways of prudence?

Evadne

    In valor: I shall lie with my husband in death.

Iphis

    You speak in sickly riddles. What is this?

Evadne

    I rush to the pyre of fallen Capaneus.   1065

Iphis

    My daughter! Do not speak that word to many.

Evadne

    I want it known by everyone in Argos.

Iphis

    I shall not suffer you to do this thing.

Evadne

    No matter, I am beyond the reach of your hand.
    My body falls! a flight not dear to you   1070
    But to me and the husband who will burn with me.

                              (She leaps into the pyre.)

Chorus

    Woman! Terrible the deed you brought to pass!

Iphis

    Daughters of Argos! I am ruined, doomed.

Chorus

    Having borne this heavy woe,
    Alas! you will grieve to see
    Her wildly daring deed.   1075

Iphis

The world holds no more miserable man.

Chorus

What suffering is yours! A part of Oedipus' doom
Has befallen you, old sire, and me and my poor city.

Iphis

In grief I ask: Why cannot mortals be   1080
Twice young, then reach old age a second time?
If anything goes wrong at home, we right it
By afterthoughts; but not so with a life.
If youth and age came twice, a double life   1085
Would be our lot, and we could set things right
No matter what mistakes were made. When I saw others
With families, I became an adorer of children
And sorely longed for some to call my own.
If I had come to this experience
With children, and known what it is for a father to lose them, 1090
Never would I have reached the point of woe
Where now I stand: to have started into life
A noble youth, and then be robbed of him.
And now, in my wretchedness, what shall I do?
Return to my house, to see the emptiness   1095
Of many rooms, and a hopeless round of living?
Or shall I go where Capaneus once dwelt?
What a delight that was, when I had this child!
But now she is no more—she who would draw   1100
My cheek to her lips and clasp my head in her hands.
To an old father, nothing is more sweet
Than a daughter. Boys are more spirited, but their ways
Are not so tender. Quickly, take me home
And give me to the dark, to starve until   1105
My aged frame is wasted and I rot.
What will I gain by touching my child's bones?
O harsh old age! How loathsome is your reign!

How I hate those who want to stretch life out,
Counting on meats and drinks and magic spells   1110
To turn the stream aside and stave off death.
When useless to the world, they ought to die:
Away with them! Let them leave it to the young.

(*The ashes of the fallen chiefs are brought in.*)

Chorus

Look, look! Alas! They are bringing
The bones of my children who perished.
Attendants, take them from a weak old woman.   1115
Grief for my children has robbed me of my strength.
I have been alive for many lengths of time
And many woes have made me melt in tears.
What greater pain can mortals feel than this: 1120
To see their children dead before their eyes?

Boys

Sorrowful mothers! Out of the fire
I bring, I bring my father's limbs;
A weight not weightless, so great is my grief   1125
As I gather my all in a little space.

Chorus

Alas, alas! Why do you bring
Tears for the mother whom the fallen loved?
A little heap of dust instead of bodies   1130
Once glorious in Mycenae?

Boys

You are childless! childless! and I,
Having lost my unhappy father, will dwell
An orphan in a house of loss,
Cut off from the man who gave me life.

Chorus

Alas, alas! Where is the labor   1135
Spent on my children? Where, the reward of childbirth,

A mother's care, sleepless devotion of eyes,
The loving kiss on the face?

Boys

They have gone, they are no more. Alas, my father!
They have gone.   1140

Chorus

The air holds them now,
Crumbled to dust in the fire;
They have winged their way to Hades.

Boys

Father, I beg you, hear your children's cries!
Shall I ever set my shield against your foes,
Making your murder engender death? May that day come!   1145
If God is willing, justice will be done
For our fathers.

Chorus

This evil sleeps not yet.
It grieves me. I have had enough
Ill chance, enough of woe.

Boys

Some day Asopus' gleam will welcome me   1150
As I march in the bronze armor of Danaus' sons
On a campaign to demand revenge for my fallen father.
Still I seem to see you, father, before my eyes—

Chorus

Planting your kiss, so loved, upon my cheek.

Boys

But your encouraging words   1155
Are borne away on the air.

Chorus

He left woe to us both: your mother,
And you, whom grief for your father will never leave.

Boys

I bear so great a burden that it has destroyed me.

Chorus

Come, let me lay the dear dust close to my breast.   1160

Boys

Oh, piteous words! I weep
To hear them; they pierce my heart.

Chorus

Child, you have gone: never again
Shall I see you, idol of your beloved mother.

Theseus

Adrastus! Women of the race of Argos!   1165
You see these youths, holding in their hands
The bodies of their fathers, noble men
Whom I took up for burial. To them
I and the city now present the ashes.
You, who behold what you have gained from me,   1170
Must keep this act in grateful recollection,
And tell your children constantly to honor
This city, handing down from son to son
The memory of answered prayers. Zeus
And the gods in heaven know the kindnesses   1175
Of which we thought you worthy. Go in peace.

Adrastus

Theseus, we are aware of all the good
You have done the land of Argos, in its need

Of benefactors, and our gratitude
Will never fade. We have been nobly treated
By you, and owe you action in return.

Theseus

How can I be of further service to you?   1180

Adrastus

By faring well, as you and your city deserve.

Theseus

We shall; and may you have the same good fortune.

(*Athene appears*, ex machina.)

Athene

Theseus, hear what I, Athene, tell you.
There is a duty that you must perform
To help the city now. Do not intrust   1185
These bones to the boys, to take to the land of Argos,
Releasing them so lightly. First exact
An oath, in compensation for the efforts
You and the city have made. Adrastus here
Must swear—he has authority, as king,
To take an oath on behalf of all the land   1190
Of Danaus' sons. And this shall be the oath:
"Argos will never move against this country
In hostile panoply. If others try
To invade it, she will hinder them by arms."
If they forsake the oath and come, then pray
That the Argive land may fall again to ruin.   1195
Now hear me name the vessel for the blood
From the rite you must perform. You have
Inside your house a tripod with feet of bronze.
After destroying Ilium's foundations
Long years ago, Heracles, going forth
On another labor, bade you set that vessel   1200

On the altar of Apollo. Over it
You must cut the throats of three sheep, and inscribe
The oath on the hollow of the tripod; then
Present it to the god who has charge of Delphi,
To be preserved in memory of the oath
And as witness to it in the eyes of Hellas.

The sharp-edged knife, with which you will perform   1205
The sacrifice and deal the death-wound, you must bury
Deep in the earth, here, beside the seven
Pyres of the fallen. Then, if the Argives ever
Move on the city, the knife, revealed, will work
Fear in their hearts, and an evil journey home.

When this is done, you must send the dead from the land,   1210
And dedicate a shrine of the Isthmian goddess
Beside the triple crossroads, where the bodies
Were purified by fire. These are my words
To you. To the sons of the Argives, I proclaim:
When you are men you will sack Ismenus' city,
Avenging the murder of your fallen fathers.   1215
You, Aigialeus, will take your father's place
As a young campaigner, and you, the son of Tydeus
From Aetolia, named Diomedes by your father.
No sooner shall you get your beards than march
A mighty force of bronze-clad Danaids   1220
Against the Thebans' seven-mouthed walls. Your coming
Will bring them sorrow—lion-cubs you are,
True-bred sackers of cities! This shall befall:
Hellas will know you as the Sons of Sons,
A theme of future song. So great will be   1225
Your expedition, favored by the gods.

Theseus

I shall obey your orders, Queen Athene!
You have corrected me; I err no more.
Now I shall bind this man to me by oath.
Only, I pray you, set me in the right path;

So long as you mean kindly to the city,
Our life will be secure to the end of time.

Chorus

Now let us go, Adrastus, and give our word
To this man and his town, whose deeds for us
Deserve the highest honors we can give.

ORESTES

Translated by William Arrowsmith

- most tragic Grk. play.
- far removed from classical form of Grk. trag.
- parady of Grk. trag.

INTRODUCTION TO ORESTES

TRAGIC in tone, melodramatic in incident and technique, by sudden wrenching turns savage, tender, grotesque, and even comic, combining sheer theatrical virtuosity with puzzling structural violence and a swamping bitterness of spirit, the *Orestes* has long been an unpopular and neglected play, almost an unread one. Undeservedly so, I think; but like so many Euripidean plays, *Orestes* has had to pay the price for affronting the pat handbook theories of the well-constructed Greek play, and its very "queerness" and bravura of bitterness have seemed to violate both the idea of tragedy and tragic dignity itself. Actually, like Shakespeare's *Troilus and Cressida*, the *Orestes* is that rare thing, a work which fits no category or ready-made genre but whose real power and odd brilliance demand a place and indict the theories which oust it from serious consideration. But so long as the standard image of the Greek play remains that of the tense and archaic ordered calm and balanced harmony of Sophoclean folklore, a play of "howling spiritual lunacy" like the *Orestes* must appear an unwelcome and unsettling freak.

What we get in the *Orestes* is, in fact, very much like what we get in *Troilus and Cressida*: tragedy utterly without affirmation, an image of heroic action seen as botched, disfigured, and sick, carried along by the machinery and slogans of heroic action in a steady crescendo of biting irony and the rage of exposure. It is neither a satire on heroic tragedy, however, nor a mere melodramatic perversion, but a kind of negative tragedy of total turbulence, deriving its real power from the exposure of the aching disparity between the ideal and the real, dooming all possibility of order and admitting dignity only as the agonizing absence by which the degree of depravity is to be judged. If, in the end, nothing but the sense of bitterness and alienation survives the corrosive effect of the action, the intensity of that experience in a world of impending disaster is in itself the bedrock of the tragic. Out of balance perhaps, distorted by a bitterness so pervasive that it seems at times almost gratuitous, it is nevertheless the anguished, despairing portrayal of a society taken in the act of self-betrayal and the defeat of political commitment.

In its material, the *Orestes* is almost entirely free invention, an imaginative rendering of the events which follow the murder of Clytemnestra by her children. Dramatically, the unifying motif of the play is the gradual exposure of the real criminal depravity of Orestes and his accomplices, an exposure made possible by a typical and deliberate piece of Euripidean anachronizing. In play after play, that is, Euripides uproots a myth from the cultural context of a remote and different time and intrudes it forcibly into a contemporary world, thereby altering its motives, its characters, and its meaning. By so doing, he effectively contrasts the ideal with the operative values of his own society. The *Orestes*, though freely invented, observes the same technique. Whereas, for instance, in the *Oresteia* of Aeschylus, Orestes' murder of his mother is the source from which the institution of civil justice flows, in the Euripidean play Orestes' matricide is set in a context where civil justice already exists. The consequence of this anachronism is to throw the whole burden of the cultural disparity upon the character of Orestes, a burden which makes him either suspect or criminal. He murders his mother, that is, in the everyday world of the audience, and the audience is therefore compelled to judge him as a man who murdered when he might have had recourse to the courts. True, he may have obeyed the command of Apollo, but, by virtue of the same anachronizing process, Apollo is here transformed from a cool and infallible Olympian into the interested and suspect god of contemporary Delphian politics, neither impartial nor infallible nor even godlike. But once shorn of his legendary aura of heroism and his justifying necessity, Orestes is revealed in action as sick, brutal, cowardly, and weak, redeemed only by his tenderness for the stronger sister and friend who dominate him and push him on to murder.

In itself the exposure of Orestes' criminal nature is both gradual and dramatic. Indeed, through the first half of the play, Euripides allows Orestes to profit from his reputed heroism and necessity, and, with the exception of several savage lapses which prepare the way for the exposure to come, he is presented as a more or less sympathetic figure. Thus everybody pities him as the suffering victim of a callous god; all blame Apollo as the true culprit, and even the trenchant remarks of Tyndareus and Menelaus are half elided because Tyndareus is made vindictive and Menelaus opportunistic. Orestes himself disarms condemnation by cleanly admitting his guilt at one point (by a forceful irony he is most sane when apparently most mad, and maddest when he is at his most lucid); and his own sickness and desperation in the face of Menelaus' abandonment of him operate insensibly to palliate or excuse his conduct. But suddenly with the decision to murder Helen and take Hermione as hostage, his true criminal nature is revealed: murder, we see now, was always in his heart, for these actions are commanded by no god but are born of desperation, spite, and hatred. And then, point for point, the depravity and cowardice which move him are exposed. Thus the man who could taunt his mother with cowardice for not having killed herself when taken in adultery willingly contemplates two more murders to save his own life, while, in pointed reversal and parody of his own cowardly lust to live and his sneers at Menelaus' cowardice, he brutally plays cat-and-mouse with a cowering, defenseless Trojan slave. And so by the end of the play, along with Electra and Pylades, he stands nakedly exposed as the degenerate heir of a great house, willing to bring down his accomplices, his innocent victim, and his house in his own ruin.

But everywhere, in the situations, in the characters, the bitterness is unrelieved, the quality of nightmare pervasive. Thus with the single exception of Hermione, a mere pawn whose compassion is typically exploited by the brutal Electra, there is not a good character in the play. Helen herself, vain of her beauty still, is shallow, selfish, and tactless and, like Orestes, shirks responsibility by blaming the gods for her conduct. Pylades (whom an insane scholiast referred to as the only good character of the play) is a monster of perverted loyalty, the exact foil to Menelaus, a man who is not even permitted the luxury of a struggle between duty and greed but is presented as a straightforward demagogue, treacherous and corrupt. Tyndareus, it is true, is permitted the only valid insight into the murder of Clytemnestra and its alternative, but his vindictiveness and harshness (he deserves comparison to Pheres in the *Alcestis*) obscure his own insight, and finally he betrays even his devotion to precedent and law in his conduct at Orestes' trial. Except for her loyalty and devotion to her brother, Electra is a piece of complete viciousness, stubborn in spite and malice with the bitterness born of envy and resentful virginity. The foolish messenger who reports the trial is, of course, *parti pris* and warped by the disease of demented loyalty that pervades the play, while the pathetic and ridiculous Phrygian slave is no more than a comic messenger designed, in his whirling helplessness and terror, to stress Orestes' brutality and perhaps to satirize contemporary Persia. The same warping that extends to all the characters extends also to all the situations, moral and political, of the play. Thus even the possibility of justice is precluded in the messenger's portrayal of the Argive assembly, dominated by demagogues and crossed by political motives that have nothing to do with justice. And so too all the parties to the action are defined either by inhuman devotion to sound principle, by patent treachery, or by nightmare loyalty of complicity or stupidity, and slowly, inexorably, all moral terms are either inverted or emptied of their meaning.

With great vividness the final tableau crowns the nightmare. On the roof of his own palace in the lurid light of smoking torches Orestes with Pylades beside him holds a drawn sword at Hermione's throat; farther back stands Electra with blazing torches, on the point of firing the roof, while below, in petrified horror, stand Menelaus and his men watching. The impasse is complete; in any natural world the whole cumulative experience of the play points unmistakably to disaster. But then, suddenly, incredibly, Apollo appears, halts the violence, and methodically hands out their known mythical futures to all the characters. In no other extant Greek play does a part of a play stand in more glaring contrast to the whole than it does here; in no other play are the futures of the characters made to clash so violently with their portrayal and development in the play. Thus, says Apollo, Orestes will marry Hermione (and we must imagine an insane *pas de deux* as Orestes drops his sword and embraces his victim); Pylades will marry Electra and live in happiness (but how could this marriage be happy, one wonders); and finally, and most incredible of all, Helen—the same shallow, tactless, empty-headed Helen of the play—is exhibited by Apollo as nothing less than a goddess, "enthroned forever, a star for sailors."

How is this strange epiphany to be understood? The stressed contradictions between it and the play proper rule out any ordinary *deus ex machina* intervening to save an impossible situation, as they equally rule out the common notion that Euripides has introduced Apollo to salvage a botched play. And while it is certainly true that Apollo's arrangements show a degree of stupidity rare even in a Euripidean god and operate to arraign the god who announces them, this hardly seems enough. What we have here, I think, is a transparent tour de force, an apparent resolution which in fact resolves nothing, the illusion of a *deus ex machina* intervening to stop the terrible momentum of the play by means of a solution so inadequate and so unreal by contrast with the created reality of the play that it is doomed into insignificance. The resolution, that is, is so designed as to be merely an apparent resolution: if the experience of the play is a real one, what remains after Apollo leaves is not the taste of the happy ending but the image of total disaster: the burning palace, the dead girl, the screaming mob, and the degenerate heirs dying in the arson of their own hatred. Or so I see it. As so often, Euripides has here juxtaposed two conflicting realities—one, the harsh irrefutable reality of experience the play makes, the other, the storied reality of myth and "things as they are said to be"—and left them there, without bridge, without explanation, without resolution. But here the violence of contrast is without parallel, almost as though Euripides had deliberately inverted the *deus ex machina* to show precisely that *no* solution was possible; not even a god could halt the momentum of these forces in their sweep toward inevitable disaster. The magician waves his wand, but the nightmare survives the magic; the discord outlasts both the coda and the concert. As a previous translator shrewdly remarks, "Apollo speaks with the voice of a cracked phonograph-record."

The *Orestes* can be accurately dated to the year 408 B.C., that is, just a year or so before Euripides, old, embittered, and disillusioned with Athens, withdrew in voluntary exile to Macedon, where he died a few years later. The political climate of the play itself graphically represents the state of affairs in Athens, and, presumptuous or not, I am tempted to see in the play Euripides' prophetic image of the final destruction of Athens and Hellas, or that Hellas to which a civilized man could still give his full commitment. It is a simple and a common symbolism: the great old house, cursed by a long history of fratricidal blood and war, brought down in destruction by its degenerate heirs. The final tableau is the direct prophecy of disaster, complete, awful, and inevitable, while Apollo intervenes only as an impossible wish, a futile hope, or a simple change of scene from a vision that cannot be brooked or seen for long because it is the direct vision of despair, the hopeless future.

CHARACTERS

Electra

Helen

most tragic + innocent Hermione, daughter of Menelaus and Helen
char. of all plays

Chorus of women of Argos

Orestes — *his rationality makes him scary. he enjoys killing*

Menelaus

Tyndareus, father of Helen and Clytemnestra

Pylades

Messenger

Phrygian slave

Apollo

For N. O. Brown

Apes enim ego divinas bestias puto, quae mel vomunt, etiam si dicuntor illud a Iove afferre; ideo autem pungunt, quia ubicunque dulce est, ibi et acidum invenies.

— internal motivation is more prominent in char.
— resp. for char. actions is partially transferred to and.
and. angry.

ORESTES

SCENE: *Before the palace of Agamemnon in Argos, six days after the murder of Clytemnestra. Near the door, huddled under blankets on a pallet, lies Orestes asleep. Electra, an embittered and exhausted woman, rises from the bedside to speak the prologue.*

Electra

There is no form of anguish with a name—
no suffering, no fate, no fall
inflicted by heaven, however terrible—
whose tortures human nature could not bear
or might not have to bear.
                  I think of Tantalus,   5
born—or so they say—the son of Zeus himself
and blessed by birth and luck as few men are:
happy Tantalus. . . .
            I do not mock his fall,
and yet that same Tantalus now writhes and trembles
in terror of the rock that overhangs his head,
though even as a man he sat as honored equal
at the table of the gods, but could not hold his tongue,   10
being sick with pride.
             Or so the legend goes.
I do not know.
         The son of Tantalus was Pelops,
father of Atreus for whom the weaving Fates
wove the threads of war, a war with his own brother,
Thyestes—
        But why should I linger on the horrors
of my house?
        Atreus feasted him on his murdered sons.   15
I pass over, in the interests of decorum,
the succeeding years.

                              By Aërope, however,
Atreus became the father of two sons,
Menelaus and famous Agamemnon—
if what he had was fame.

                              The wife of Menelaus
was Helen, whom the gods in heaven themselves   20
despise, while Agamemnon married Clytemnestra
in a marriage that became the scandal of Hellas.
By her he had three daughters—myself
and my two sisters, Chrysothemis and Iphigenia—
and one son, Orestes there. All of us his children
by that one wife—I cannot call her mother—
who snared her husband in the meshes of a net   25
and murdered him.

                              I leave it to the world
to guess her motive. It is no topic for a virgin
like myself.

                              And why repeat the old charges
against Apollo?

                              The world knows all too well
how he pushed Orestes on to murder the mother
who gave him birth, that act of matricide   30
which wins, it seems, something less than approval
in men's eyes. But persuaded by the god, he killed,
and I did all a woman could to help him,
while Pylades, our friend, shared the crime
with us.

                              After the murder Orestes collapsed   35
to bed. There he lies, wasted by raging fever
and whirled on to madness by his mother's blood—
I dare not breathe the name of those Eumenides
who pursue him now, hounding him with terror.
   Six days now since our mother's murder;
six days since we sent her body to the fire.   40
And all that time he has not tasted food
or wet his lips or bathed, but lies there

huddled in the blankets. When the fever lifts,
he turns lucid and cries; then suddenly, madly,
bolts from the bed like an untamed colt   45
bucking the bridle.
     Meanwhile the people of Argos
have passed a decree, declaring us matricides
and outlaws, forbidding anyone to speak to us
or give us shelter.
     But this day decides our fate.
On this day the city of Argos assembles
to vote whether we shall live or die,
and, if we die, then the manner of our death—   50
by stoning or the sword.
     One single hope is left.
Our uncle Menelaus has just come home
from Troy. His fleet fills the harbor at Nauplia,
riding at anchor just offshore after all those years
out of Troy and lost at sea.
     Helen, however—   55
who now styles herself "the queen of sorrows"—
was so terrified that she might be seen
and stoned by the fathers of those who died at Troy,
that Menelaus sent her on ahead last night
under cover of darkness.
     She is here now,   60
inside the house, weeping over her sister's death
and the ruin of our house.
     She has, I might add,
some consolation—her daughter, Hermione,
whom Menelaus, before he sailed for Troy,
brought from Sparta and intrusted to my mother's care.   65
So *she*, at least, has some comfort left;
she can afford to forget.
     But we cannot.
I stand here now, watching the road in the hope
of seeing Menelaus on his way.

Unless he helps us now, unless he rescues us,
then we must die. Nothing is so weak
and helpless as a fallen house.   70

(Enter Helen from the palace. She is middle-aged but still hand-
    some and still vain of her beauty. She carries a pitcher for
    libations and several small clippings of her own hair.)

Helen

                            There you are.
Oh, dear Electra, Clytemnestra's daughter....
But you poor girl, still not married!
And how are you, dear?

                        And how is poor Orestes?
How you must suffer!

                    I can't believe it.
To murder your own mother! How horrible!
But there, dear, I know. You were not to blame.   75
The real culprit was Apollo. And for my part,
I can see no reason on earth for shunning you,
none at all.

            And yet, poor Clytemnestra—
my only sister!

                And to think I sailed for Troy
on that tragic voyage without even seeing her!
Some god must have driven me mad.

                                And now she is gone,
and I am the only one left to mourn for her....   80

Electra

Why tell you, Helen, what you can see for yourself?
There lies the wreck of Agamemnon's son,
while I sit here at my sleepless post
beside his corpse. But for a little breath,
a corpse is what he is.

                        I do not complain   85
on his account.

But *you*, you and your husband,
with your reek of triumph, your smug success,
you come to us in our utter misery—

Helen

When did he collapse?

Electra

                The day he spilt
his mother's blood.

Helen

                One day and two deaths,   90
a mother and her son.

Electra

                Yes, he killed himself
when he killed her.

Helen

                I wanted to ask, niece,
could you do me a favor?

Electra

                        I have a moment free.
He is sleeping now and does not need my care.

Helen

Would you go for me to my sister's grave?   95

Electra

  What!
        You want *me* to go to my mother's grave?
But why?

Helen

                To pour libations on her grave
and leave this little clipping of my hair.

Electra

But she was *your* sister, You should go yourself.

Helen

I am afraid, ashamed to show my face
in Argos.

Electra

         This repentance comes a little late.
Where was your shame when you ran away from home
and left your husband?

Helen

                Spoken with more truth than kindness   100

to your aunt.

Electra

          Then why are you ashamed?

Helen

The fathers of those who died fighting at Troy—
they frighten me.

Electra

           Well they might. You are a byword

here in Argos.

Helen

          Please go. Save me.

Electra

                 No.

I could not bear the sight of my mother's grave.   105

Helen

 But it wouldn't do to send a servant there.

Electra

Then send Hermione.

Helen

                      Send an unmarried girl
on an errand in public?

Electra

                      It is her duty.
She owes it to my mother for bringing her up.

Helen

  Quite right, my dear.

                     An excellent suggestion.   110
I'll call her out.

                          (Helen calls into the palace.)

                Hermione, dear,
come outside.

            (Hermione, a young girl, emerges from the palace.)

            Now do exactly what I say.
Take this libation and these clippings of hair
and go to Clytemnestra's grave. Stand there
and pour this mixture of honey, milk, and wine   115
over the grave and, as you pour, repeat
these words:
          "Your loving sister Helen,
prevented by fear of the Argives from coming
to your grave in person, sends you these gifts."
Then implore her to be gracious to us all,
to my husband and me and these poor children   120
whom Apollo has destroyed. Promise her besides
that I will labor to perform, like a good sister,
all the dues and rites of the gods below.
Now go, dear. Hurry there, make your offering
and then come back as quickly as you can.   125

    (Exit Hermione with offerings. Helen retires into the palace.)

Electra

  Oh, what a vileness human beauty is,
corroding, corrupting everything it touches!

What a curse, and yet the glory of the good. . . .
Did you see how she clipped the merest tips of her curls,
so stingy with her loveliness?

       The same old Helen.

O gods, how can you help loathing this woman,   130
this monster who has ruined my brother and me
and all Hellas?

     (*Slowly and silently the Chorus of Argive women*
           begins to file into the orchestra.)

    But here they come again,
those loving friends who keep their watch with me
and mourn.

     But if they wake him from his sleep,
if I must see my brother going mad   135
once more, I shall cry out my eyes with grief.

         (*To Chorus.*)

Walk softly, friends. Gently. . . .

       Hush.

Quiet, quiet. Not a step or sound,
not a whisper.

     Your kindness is well meant,
but if you wake him now, I shall die. . . .

Chorus

  Hush.

     Not a sound. Tiptoe softly.   140
  Barely, barely touch the ground.

Electra

  Back, back from the bed!

Chorus

  Back we go.

Electra

     Your music, friends—
  keep it down, flute it low,   145

as soft as gentle breath may go
down the stem of your reed.

Chorus

There. Hear it, so soft,
so low—

Electra

       No. Lower still.
Now tiptoe to me, softly, so—
and tell me why you come   150
now that he sleeps at last,
he sleeps. . . .

Chorus

       How now? How?
Will he live? Will he die?

Electra

He breathes, he breathes—
his breath comes slow.   155

Chorus

          O gods,
help him to live!

Electra

        If his eyes
so much as move, you kill him. . . .
O gods, he sleeps, he sleeps
at last.

Chorus

       Condemned to suffer   160
for a god's command!
How terribly he suffers—

Electra

Evil the act, evil the god,
that evil day Apollo on his throne

commanded my mother's death,
murder for murder!

Chorus
                    Look, look!
In the bed—his body stirring!

Electra
    Hush.
            In god's name, be still!
Look, your cries have wakened him,
have broken his sleep—

Chorus
                        No, no.
He sleeps, he sleeps....

Electra
                    Back,
back from the bed.   170
                    Not a sound,
not a cry.
            For god's sake, go!
Chorus
Now he sleeps.

Electra
                Then let him sleep.
Chorus
    O night, mother of mercy,
    blessed night,
    who gives to human anguish   175
    the lovely gift of sleep,
    rise,
        rise from your abyss
    and soar to Agamemnon's house,
    where all is ruin,
                    all is loss!   180

Electra

Hush.

No more.

In the name of god, be still,
be still! No more mourning,
or you rob him of his peace,
this gracious peace of sleep—   185

Chorus

Where, where will it end?

Electra

Death, death.

What is left
but death? He refuses food.

Chorus

Then death must come.   190

Electra

Yes,
and I must die with him.
Apollo killed us both,
vengeance for our mother
when our father's ghost cried out
against our mother, *blood, blood!*

Chorus

Just the act, crime unjust.
Right and wrong confounded
in a single act.

Electra

O Mother,
mother who gave me birth,
who killed and was killed,   195
you slew your husband,
you killed your children too.

By your death we died.
We are the living dead.   200
You are dust and ashes,
while I, a living ghost,
dead to this sunlit world,
stalk with withered life,
childless, unmarried,   205
crying my sorrow, lost,
alone in the endless night.

Coryphaeus

Electra! Look and see if your brother has died
while we were mourning. He lies so still now—   210
I do not like it.

       (*Orestes suddenly stirs and wakes.*)

Orestes

     O sweet wizard sleep,
savior of the sick, dear loveliness
that came to me in my worst need of you!
O goddess sleep, goddess of forgetting,
to whom the unhappy make their prayers,
how skilled, how wise....

       But what happened?
Who put me here?

    I somehow—can't remember....   215

Electra

How happy it made me to see you fall asleep
at last.

    Should I raise your head, dear?

Orestes

Yes, please. Help me up.

      Now wipe away
this crust of froth around my mouth and eyes.   220

Electra

> This service is sweet, and I do it gladly,
> nursing my brother with a sister's love.

Orestes

> > > > Sit here
> beside me. Now brush this matted hair
> from my eyes so I can see.

Electra

> > > Oh, that poor head!
> And look at your hair, so snarled and dirty....   225
> And those tangled curls!

Orestes

> > > > (*Suddenly slumping back.*)
> > > Let me lie back down.
> That's better. After these attacks of fever,
> my arms and legs seem somehow limp....

Electra

> > > > Lie down
> and don't move. Sick men must stay in bed.
> Frustrating, I know, but it can't be helped.   230

Orestes

> Prop me up again. Now turn me around.
> What a nuisance I am in my helplessness.

Electra

> Would you like to try walking a step or two?
> The change may do you good.

Orestes

> > > With all my heart.
> Right now even the suggestion of health,   235
> however false, would be welcome.

Electra

Listen, Orestes,

I have something to say. But you must listen now
while your mind is clear and the Furies leave you free.

Orestes

If your news is good news, by all means tell me.
If not, I have troubles enough.   240

Electra

Listen then.

Our uncle Menelaus is *here*, in Argos.
His fleet lies at anchor at Nauplia.

Orestes

What?

Is it true? Then this darkness has a dawn!
Our uncle here? The man for whom our father
did so much?

Electra

Here in person. And the proof   245

is Helen. He has brought her home from Troy.

Orestes

I would envy him more if he'd left her there.
If Helen is here, he has brought his trouble home.

Electra

Poor Tyndareus.

What daughters he fathered!

Helen and our mother, Clytemnestra!
And both disgraced him in the eyes of Hellas.   250

Orestes

Take care that you act differently: *you* can.
I mean chastity of heart as well as word.

(*Orestes suddenly starts wildly up, then cowers
back, his eyes wild with terror.*)

Electra

   Orestes!

        O gods, his eyes are whirling!

Oh no! *No!*

          Help! He is going mad!

Orestes

   No, *Mother!*

        For god's sake, Mother,   255

keep them away, those bitches with bloodshot eyes,

those writhing snakes!

          Help! They're coming,

they're leaping at me—

       (*Electra seizes him by the arm and leads him to his bed.*)

Electra

          Please, go back to bed.

There is nothing there, nothing at all.

These are only phantoms in your mind.

Orestes

   Apollo, save me!

         They want to kill me,   260

those bitches with gorgon eyes, those goddesses

of hell!

Electra

      No, stop! I won't let you go.

You must not go. I'll hold you by the waist

and keep you here by force!

        (*She grasps Orestes around his waist and*

             holds him down on the bed.)

Orestes

        Let me go!

I know *you.* You're one of my Furies too!

You're holding me down to hurl me into hell!   265

     (*He breaks loose, shoves her aside, and springs up.*)

Electra

    What can I do?
                How can I help him now?
Nothing human can save him now. No,
heaven hates us both.

Orestes

                      Get me my horn-tipped bow,
the bow Apollo gave me to scare these bitches off   270
if they threatened me with madness.

               (*Electra hands him the bow and quiver. Orestes
                    notches an arrow and draws the bow.*)

                          Vanish, demons!
Goddesses you may be, but unless you go,
this human hand shall draw your blood.
                        Damn it, go!

Ignore me, do you?
                Do you see this bow
already drawn, this arrow notched and ready?
What? Still here?
               Vanish, spread your wings!   275
Skim the air, will you! Go hound Apollo,
accuse his oracle. But go! Go!

     (*He suddenly stumbles, dropping his bow, and sanity returns.*)
What was I saying?
               And why am I panting so?
What am I doing here, out of bed?
                  But wait—
I remember now—a great storm, the waves crashing—
but now this calm—this peace. . . .

          (*He catches sight of Electra, her face hidden in
             her robes, sobbing softly by the bed.*)
                 Why are you crying?   280
Why do you hide your face?

Oh, my poor sister,
how wrong it is that what I have to suffer,
this sickness, this madness, should hurt you too
and cause you shame.

Please, please don't cry,
not on my account.

Let me bear the shame.
I know, you consented to the murder too,
but I killed, not you.

No—
I accuse Apollo. The god is the guilty one.   285
It was he who drove me to this dreadful crime,
he and his words, egging me, encouraging me,
all words, no action.

I think now
if I had asked my dead father at the time
if I should kill her, he would have begged me,
gone down on his knees before me, and pleaded,   290
implored me not to take my mother's life.
What had we to gain by murdering her?
Her death could never bring him back to life
and I, by killing her, would have to suffer
as I suffer now.

It seems so hopeless, dear,
I know.

But lift your head; do not cry.   295
And sometimes when you see me morbid and depressed,
comfort me and calm me, and I in turn,
when you despair, will comfort you with love.
For love is all we have, the only way
that each can help the other.

Now go inside.   300
Bathe and eat and give those tired eyes
their needed sleep. If you should leave me now,
if you fall ill yourself from nursing me,
then I am dead. You are all my help;   305
you are my hope.

Electra

I could never leave you.
Live or die, I live or die with you, Orestes.
For you are my hope too, as I am yours.
What am I without you?

A woman,
brotherless, fatherless, friendless, alone
and helpless.

But since you think it best, dear,   310
I'll go inside.

But you go back to bed
and rest. Above all else, try to stay calm
and master your terror, if you can. Remember:
no getting out of bed.

Your sickness may be real
or something in your mind, but in either case,
brooding on it will not make you well.   315

(Electra enters the palace. Orestes lies down on the bed.)

Chorus

Goddesses of terror,
runners on the wind,
revelers of sorrow
whose rites are tears!   320
Women of darkness,
Eumenides whose wings
shiver the taut air,
demanding blood,
avengers of murder,
we implore you—
release this boy,
Agamemnon's son,   325
from madness of murder,
the blood that whirls him on!
Pity, pity we cry,
pity for the crime,

murder that came on,
drove from Apollo's throne,
the god's command to kill
breaking the hushed, the holy air,
with the word of blood—
blood drenching the shrine   330
of Delphi—
            Delphi,
holiest of holies
and navel of the world!

O Zeus, what mercy?
What mercy for this boy
on whom the fiend descends,   335
the spirit of vengeance
for his mother's blood,
savage spirit, driving on his house
in gust on gust of grief,
blood and the madness of blood,
madness born of murder?
We mourn for this boy;
we grieve for this house.

Happiness is brief.
It will not stay.
God batters at its sails,   340
the tossing seas are wild;
anguish like a wind
whips down,
sorrow strikes,
swamps the scudding ship
and happiness goes down
and glory sinks.
            And yet
what other house, what name   345
more deserves our praise

than this line of glory,
born of Tantalus and Zeus?

And now behold the king—
royal Menelaus
whose magnificence declares   350
the blood of Tantalus!

> (*Enter Menelaus, with great magnificence and pomp,*
> *followed by a large retinue.*)

All hail, the king!
Hail to the king who led
a thousand ships to Troy,
and did with heaven's help
all he vowed to do!   355
Hail him! Glory and success
go beside the king!

Menelaus

Home from Troy at last.
        How happy I am
to see this house once more—
        but also sad,
for never have I seen a house more hedged about
by suffering than this.
        I was putting in to shore
near Cape Malea when I first heard the news   360
of Agamemnon's murder at the hands of his wife.
For Glaucus, the god of sailors and a prophet
who does not lie, suddenly rose from the sea
in clear view of the ships and cried:
        "Menelaus,   365
your brother lies dying in his bath,
the last bath his wife will ever give him."
My crew and I alike burst into tears
at this dreadful news.

Well, so we reached Nauplia.
My wife Helen came on ahead at night,   370
and I was looking forward to seeing Orestes and his mother,
thinking, of course, that they at least were well,
when some sailor told me of the shocking murder
of Clytemnestra.

Can you tell me, women,   375
where I might find my nephew Orestes?
He was still a baby in his mother's arms
when I left for Troy, so I would not know him
if I saw him.

Orestes

Here I am, Menelaus:
Orestes in person, and only too willing   380
to tell you the story of my sufferings.
But first I fall before you on my knees
and beg you, implore you, to rescue me from death.
You come in the nick of time.

Menelaus

Gods in heaven,   385
is this some corpse I see?

Orestes

More dead than living,
I admit. Still alive, but dead of my despair.

Menelaus

And that wild, matted hair—how horrible you look!

Orestes

It is my crimes, not my looks, that torture me.

Menelaus

That awful stare—and those dry, cold eyes. . . .

Orestes

My body is dead. I am the name it had.   390

Menelaus

But I did not expect this—alteration.

Orestes

I am a murderer. I murdered my mother.

Menelaus

So I have heard. Kindly spare me your horrors.

Orestes

I spare you—although no god spared me.

Menelaus

What is your sickness?

Orestes

                    I call it conscience.   395
The certain knowledge of wrong, the conviction of crime.

Menelaus

You speak somewhat obscurely. What do you mean?

Orestes

I mean remorse. I am sick with remorse.

Menelaus

A harsh goddess, I know. But there are cures.

Orestes

And madness too. The vengeance of my mother's blood.   400

Menelaus

When did this madness start?

Orestes

                              The very day
we built her tomb. My poor mother's tomb. . . .

Menelaus

What were you doing when the madness struck?
Were you inside or at the pyre?

Orestes

It was night.
I was standing by the pyre to gather her ashes.

Menelaus

Was there anyone there who could help you?   405

Orestes

Pylades. My accomplice in the murder.

Menelaus

But these phantoms. Can you describe them?

Orestes

I seemed to see three women, black as night—

Menelaus

Say no more. I know the spirits you mean.
I refuse to speak their name.

Orestes

You are wise.   410
They are awful.

Menelaus

And these women, you say,
hound you with madness for killing your mother?

Orestes

If you knew the torture, knew how they hounded me!

Menelaus

That criminals should suffer is hardly strange.

Orestes

There is one recourse left.

Menelaus

Suicide, you mean?

Most unwise.

Orestes

No, not that. I mean Apollo.

It was he who commanded my mother's murder.

Menelaus

A callous, unjust, and immoral order.

Orestes

We obey the gods—whoever the gods may be.

Menelaus

Apollo, despite all this, refuses to help?

Orestes

Oh, he will. In his own good time, of course. 420
Gods are slow by nature.

Menelaus

How long has it been

since your mother's death?

Orestes

Six days now.

Her pyre is still warm.

Menelaus

Only six days?

Gods, you say, are slow, but how quickly
your mother's avengers came!

Orestes

Menelaus,

I lack your clever wit. But I was—and am—
loyal to those I love.

Menelaus

What of your father?   425
Is there any help from him?

Orestes

Nothing yet.
And nothing yet means nothing ever.

Menelaus

How do you stand with the city?

Orestes

So hated
and despised that not one person in Argos
will speak to me.

Menelaus

Have your hands been cleansed
of the blood you shed?

Orestes

They shut their doors in my face.   430

Menelaus

Who is your worst enemy in Argos?

Orestes

Oeax,
Palamedes' brother. He hated my father
because of what happened at Troy.

Menelaus

I see.
He wants your death in revenge for his brother.

Orestes

Whom I never hurt. And yet his death kills me.

Menelaus

Any others? Aegisthus' men, I suppose?   435

Orestes

    Yes, they all hate me, and the city gives them
a hearing now.

Menelaus

                But will they let you keep
your father's scepter?

Orestes

                      Let me keep the scepter
when they won't let me live?

Menelaus

                            What are their plans?

Orestes

    The city is voting on our sentence today.   440

Menelaus

    What is the verdict? Banishment or death?

Orestes

    Death by stoning.

Menelaus

                Then why not try to escape?

Orestes

    We are surrounded by a ring of solid steel.

Menelaus

    Are they Argive soldiers? Or mercenaries
hired by your enemies?

Orestes

                  It comes to this: 445
everyone in Argos wants me dead.
They are unanimous.

Menelaus

              In that case, my boy,
your chances look very slim.

Orestes
                              And that is why
I turn to you.
                    You are now our only hope.
Menelaus, we are desperate. You, in contrast,
arrive in Argos at the moment of success,   450
flushed with triumph, prosperous and happy.
I implore you: share that happiness with us;
do not hoard your power and success.
Help us.
            Repay my father's services to you
by saving us. Share, if only for an hour,
our dangers and disgrace.
                              Friends show their love
in times of trouble, not in happiness.   455

Coryphaeus
Look, Menelaus:
                    Tyndareus of Sparta
on his way here, his hair shorn close
and dressed in black mourning for his daughter.

Orestes
O gods, this is the end.
                    What can I do?
Menelaus, of all the men on earth I dread to meet,   460
this is the one I dread the most, the one man
in whose presence I feel the wrenching shame
of what I did.
                    My grandfather, Tyndareus—
the man who cared for me when I was small,
who held me in his arms so tenderly—
Agamemnon's baby boy—who loved me,
he and Leda both, no less than their own sons,   465
Castor and Polydeuces.
                    They loved me,
and how have I returned their tenderness and love?

O gods, this worthlessness I am!
Where can I run?
                                    Where can I hide
from that old man's eye?

(*Enter Tyndareus, a spare, gaunt figure of great age, dressed in
mourning black. His speech is harsh, spoken with the
crabbed authority of Spartan style and
the bitterness of old age. He is
followed by attendants.*)

Tyndareus
                                    Where can I find   470
my son-in-law Menelaus, women?
I was pouring libations on my daughter's grave
when I heard the news of his arrival home
at Nauplia after those long years abroad.
Helen is also here, I understand.
Can you show me the way?
                                    I am most eager
to see him again after his long absence.   475

Menelaus
  Tyndareus!

Tyndareus
                      Menelaus, my son!

                    (*He stops short as he suddenly catches sight of Orestes.*)
Is *he* here?
                      If I had known that he was here,
I never would have come.
                                    Look at him,
Menelaus: the man who murdered his mother,
coiled like a snake at the door, those sick eyes
glowing like coals—
                                    What a loathsome sight!   480
How can you bear to speak to a *thing* like this?

Menelaus

Why not? I loved my brother. This is his son.

Tyndareus

This, Agamemnon's son? This *thing?*

Menelaus

Yes.

His son, in trouble, and I honor him.

Tyndareus

Your foreigners, I see, have taught you their ways.   485

Menelaus

It is a Greek custom, I think, to honor your kin.

Tyndareus

But not to put yourself above the laws.

Menelaus

Necessity is legislator here.
Under compulsion, no man on earth is free—
or so I hold.

Tyndareus

That is your theory then.
It is not mine and I want none of it.

Menelaus

Your age—and anger—cripple your understanding.   490

Tyndareus

Understanding, you say?
What in the name of god
does understanding have to do with *him?*
Is there some *moral* question here in dispute
between us?
If moral facts are clear to all,

if right and wrong are plain as black and white,
what man ever acted more blindly,
more stupidly, with smaller understanding
of right and wrong than this man?

                    Not once,
mind you, did he weigh the justice of his cause
or avail himself of the law and our courts for murder!   495
What should he have done?

               When his father died—
killed, I admit, by my own daughter's hand,
an atrocious crime which I do not condone
and never shall—he should have haled his mother
into court, charged her formally with murder,   500
and made her pay the penalty prescribed,
expulsion from his house.

             Legal action,
not murder. That was the course to take.
Under the circumstances, a hard choice,
true, but the course of self-control
and due respect for law, and the better choice
of two evils.

          But as things stand now,
what difference is there between him and his mother?
No, vicious as she was, if anything,
the evil he has done by killing her   505
has far surpassed her crime.

           Think again,
Menelaus.

       Suppose a wife murders her husband.
Her son then follows suit by killing her,
and his son then must have his murder too
and so on.

        Where, I want to know, can this chain   510
of murder end? Can it ever end, in fact,
since the last to kill is doomed to stand
under permanent sentence of death by revenge?

No, our ancestors handled these matters well
by banning their murderers from public sight,
forbidding them to meet or speak to anyone.
But the point is this: they purged their guilt   515
by banishment, not death. And by so doing,
they stopped that endless vicious cycle
of murder and revenge.
                          Do not mistake me.
I despise adultery and unfaithful wives,
and my daughter Clytemnestra, an adulteress
and murderess to boot, most of all.
As for your wife Helen, I loathe her too   520
and never wish to speak to her again.
Nor, I might add, do I envy you
your trip to Troy to bring your whore back home.
No sir, not my daughters, but the law:
that is my concern. There I take my stand,
defending it with all my heart and strength
against the brutal and inhuman spirit of murder
that corrupts our cities and destroys this country.   525

                    (*He turns on Orestes in fury.*)

Yes, you heard me, monster!
                        Inhuman spirit,
I said.
          Where was your pity, your humanity,
when your mother bared her breast and begged you
for her life?
              I did not see that pitiful sight,
but the very thought of it makes the tears come
to these eyes.
                One thing I know for certain: 530
heaven loathes you. These fits of madness
are the price you pay for murder; heaven itself
has made you mad. No further proof is needed.
So be warned, Menelaus.

If you help this man,
if you so much as lift a finger in his defense,
you challenge the express will of heaven.
So let him be. Let them stone him to death
or—I give you warning, sir—never set foot
in Sparta again.

         My own daughter is dead,
and she deserved to die, but it was wrong
that he should kill her.

                Except for my daughters,
I might have lived a happy man and died in peace.
But there my fortunes failed.

Coryphaeus

            Lucky that man
whose children make his happiness in life
and not his grief, the anguished disappointment
of his hopes.

Orestes

          Sir, I shrink from speaking,
knowing almost anything I say will displease you
or offend you.

          My murder of my mother was,
I admit, a crime. But in another sense,
since, by killing her, I avenged my father,
there was no crime at all.

        (*Tyndareus starts to walk away in disgust.*)

          Wait. Listen.
Let me speak. This respect I feel for your age
cripples me, shames me. If you only knew
how that white hair of yours harrows me
with shame.

         (*Tyndareus stops and listens.*)

      What else *could* I have done?
I had two duties, two clear choices,
both of them conflicting.

My father begot me,
my mother gave me birth. She was the furrow
in which his seed was sown. But without the father,
there is no birth. That being so, I thought,   555
I ought to stand by him, the true agent
of my birth and being, rather than with her
who merely brought me up.

      And then your daughter—
I blush with shame to call that woman my mother—
in a mock marriage, in the private rites of lust,
took a lover in her bed. And I hurt myself
as much as I hurt her by that admission.
But I admit it: what does it matter now?   560
Yes, Aegisthus was her lover; he was the husband
hidden in the house. And so I killed them both,
two murders, both committed for the single motive
of avenging my father.

      For this you threaten me
with stoning. But, in fact, I did a service,   565
a patriotic service.

      Tell me, what would happen
if our women decided to adopt my mother's example,
killed their husbands and then came rushing home
to their children, exposing their breasts for pity?
Why, they could murder a man for any trifle,
on any pretext. But my "crime," as you call it,   570
has stopped that practice for good or kept it
from spreading.

      I had every right to kill her.
I hated her, and I had every reason in the world
to hate.

      Gods, my poor father away from home,
a soldier fighting in war in his country's service,
and what did she do? She took a lover   575
and betrayed his bed!

      And when she was caught,

did she do the proper thing and put herself
to death?

        Not my mother. No, she murdered him
to save herself.

           I should not invoke the gods
when defending myself on a charge of murder,
but *in god's name, in the name of heaven,*
what was I supposed to do?

               Shout hurrah   580
by keeping still?

          And what would *he* have done?
Hounded me with the Furies of a father's hatred!
Or are there Furies on my mother's side,
but none to help him in his deeper hurt?
It was *you: you* destroyed me, Tyndareus.
You were the father of that woman who killed   585
my father and made a murderer of me.
And what of this?

         Odysseus had a son,
but was Telemachus compelled to kill *his* mother?
No. And why? She refused to take a lover.   590
She was loyal to Odysseus.

           And what of this?
Or have you forgotten Apollo, the god of Delphi,
navel and center of the world? The one god
whose every oracle and word mankind obeys
blindly? He *commanded* my mother's murder.
Accuse *him* of murder, then. Put *him* to death.   595
He is the culprit, not I.

         What could *I* do?
Or was he competent to command a murder,
but now incompetent to purge the guilt?
Then where *can* I go, what *can* I do,
if the god who ordered me to kill my mother
cannot, or will not, save me?

          One more thing.

Let no man say that what we did was wrong,   600
but that doing what we did, we did it
to our great cost and misery.
                              As in action,
so in marriage too. Marry, and with luck
it may go well. But when a marriage fails,
then those who marry live at home in hell.

Coryphaeus

Women by nature, it seems, were born to be   605
a great impediment and bitterness
in the lives of men.

Tyndareus

                    Since bluster is your answer,
since you insist on brazening it out
and every word you speak is said in spite,
I am even more impatient than before
to see you die.
                My purpose in coming here
was to lay some flowers on your mother's grave.   610
But now, by god, I have a deeper motive—
your death!
            I will go to the Argives myself.
They may resent it, but, by heaven, I'll hound them
until they stone your sister and you to death!
Yes, your sister too!
                    She deserves it,   615
by god, even more than you!
                            It was *she*,
that girl, who incited you against your mother,
stuffing your ears day in and day out
with her malice and venom, telling you her dreams
of Agamemnon's ghost and what he said,
tattling to you of your mother's adultery—
which I dearly hope offends the gods below   620

as much as it disgusted us on earth!
That was her effort. Yes, she worked on you
until she set this whole house on fire
with the arson of her malice.

One thing more,
Menelaus.

I warn you, if my love or hate
matter to you at all, do not oppose the gods
by rescuing this man.

No, let them stone him,   625
or—mark my words—never set foot in Sparta
again.

I warn you, do not make the mistake
of siding with outlaws and criminals like this
against god-fearing and law-abiding men.
Servants, lead me away.

> (*Exit Tyndareus, escorted by attendants. Menelaus
> begins to pace anxiously up and down.*)

Orestes

Good. Go.   630
Let Menelaus hear the rest of my appeal
uninterrupted. Spare us the nuisance
of respecting your old age.

—But, Menelaus,
why that troubled look? And why are you pacing
up and down that way?

Menelaus

Let me think.
I am trying to decide on the wisest course.   635
And, frankly, I am puzzled.

Orestes

Then postpone decision
for a while. Hear what I have to say
and then decide at leisure.

Menelaus
                    Fair enough.
There are times for keeping still and times
for speaking out. This is the time to speak.
Go ahead.

Orestes
                    Forgive me if I speak at length.   640
But the more comprehensive I can be,
the better.
                    Let me be honest, Menelaus.
It is not your money that I need. What I want
from you is what my father gave you once—
by which I do not mean money. I mean life.
Give me life and you give me something more precious   645
than money.
                    I committed a crime, and I admit it.
But right or wrong, it is only right
that you should do some wrong to help me now.
When my father mustered an army for the siege
of Troy, he also did a wrong—and yet
that wrong was generous. He did that wrong for you,
to right the wrong that your wife Helen did.   650
And wrong for wrong, you owe me that wrong now,
Menelaus.
                    Good brother that he was,
my father volunteered his life for you,
fighting as a soldier at your side
for ten long years of war. And why?
For this alone: to help you win your wife
and bring her home.
                    What you had of him,   655
I now exact of you. Fight on my behalf,
not ten long years, but one brief day.
Again, my sister Iphigenia died at Aulis
on your account. But any claim I have on you

for my sister's death, I freely waive.
Hermione may live. For as things stand now, 660
I cannot press my claim, and I forgive you
your advantage.
            But repay my father's loan;
settle your score with him by saving us.
Think: if I die, I leave my father's house
heirless, orphaned of life.
                Impossible, 665
you say?
        But surely this is just the point,
Menelaus.
          If you love us, *this* is the time
to help, *now,* when everything we have
is lost.
        Who wants help when the gods are good
and all is well? No, the man whom heaven helps
has friends enough. But now we need your help.
   All Hellas knows how much you love your wife.
I am not trying to flatter you or wheedle you, 670
but in Helen's name, I beg you—

                   (*Menelaus turns away.*)

         It is no use.
He will not help.
        But let me make one last attempt.

             (*He falls at Menelaus' feet.*)

In the name of all our house, our family,
O Uncle, my father's brother, save us now!
Imagine that my dead father in his grave 675
listens to me now, that his spirit is hovering
over you, that he himself is speaking, pleading
through my lips!
         You have seen our sufferings
and our despair, and I have begged you for my life—
life, the one hope of every man on earth,
not mine alone.

Coryphaeus
> I am only a woman,   680
> but I implore you: help them, save them.
> It lies in your power.

Menelaus
> Believe me, Orestes,
> I sympathize from the bottom of my heart.
> And nothing in this world would please me more
> than to honor that touching appeal for help.
> We are joined, besides, by a common bond of blood,
> and I am honor bound to come to your defense   685
> against your enemies, even at the cost
> of my life—obliged, in short, to do everything
> it lies in my power to do.
> God knows,
> I only wish I could.
> But it just so happens
> that I arrived in Argos in a weakened way—
> devoid of support—my allies have dwindled away—
> myself exhausted by our terrible ordeal,
> and barely able to count on even a fraction   690
> of my former friends.
> Under the circumstances—
> as I think you will agree—the obvious notion
> of beating Argos to her knees by a show of strength 695
> is quite out of the question.
> Let me be frank.
> We are weak, and therefore our weapons must be
> diplomacy and tact. Inadequate,
> I admit, but not perhaps quite hopeless.
> Whereas even to suggest a show of strength
> as a way out, given our present weakness,
> is palpable folly.
> Look at it this way, my boy.
> Mobs in their emotions are much like children,

subject to the same tantrums and fits of fury.
But this anger must be treated with great patience,
rather like a fire that gets out of control.
Hands off is best. You sit quietly by,
watching and waiting, patiently biding your time
while their fury runs its course unchecked.
With any luck, it quickly burns itself out,
and in the lull, while the wind is shifting,   700
anything you want is yours for the asking.
Anger, however, is only one of their moods;
pity is another—but precious assets both,
if you know what you're doing.
                   Now this is my plan.
I'll go and smooth matters over
with Tyndareus and the city and persuade them   705
to moderate their tone.
               As with sailing,
so with politics: make your cloth too taut,
and your ship will dip and keel, but slacken off
and trim your sails, and things head up again.
The gods, you know, resent being importuned
too much; in the same way the people dislike
being pushed or hustled. Too much zeal offends
where indirection works. And our only chance
of saving you at all lies in skill and tact,   710
not in force, as you perhaps imagine.
But these are the facts. On my own
I lack the men and strength your rescue requires;
and the Argives, I know, are not the sort of men
to be overawed by threats.
             No, if we're wise,
we will do what we must and accept the facts.   715
We have no other choice.

           (Exit Menelaus attended by his retinue.)

Orestes

You cheap traitor!
What in god's name have you ever done
but fight a war to bring your wife back home?
So now you turn your back and desert me,
do you?

This is the end, this is the last
of the house of Agamemnon.   720

My poor father—
even in his grave, deserted by his friends. . . .
And now my last hope, my only refuge
from death is lost. . . .

See, there it goes—
that traitor Menelaus was my final hope.
But wait—

Look! I see Pylades!
My best friend, Pylades, on his way   725
from Phocis!

Thank god! What a sight!
A friend, a loyal friend, in my despair.
No sailor ever saw a calm more greedily
than I now see my friend—

Pylades!

(*Enter Pylades.*)

Pylades

I seem to have reached here none too soon, Orestes.
As I was coming through town, I saw the Argives meeting   730
and with my own ears heard them discussing some proposal
to execute your sister and you.

In the name of heaven,
what has happened here? What does all this mean?

Orestes

It means this: we are ruined.

Pylades

Include me in that "we." 735
Friends share and share alike.

Orestes

That traitor Menelaus—
he betrayed my sister and me.

Pylades

I am not surprised.
A vicious husband for a vicious wife.

Orestes

By coming home
he helped my cause as much as if he'd stayed in Troy.

Pylades

Then the rumor *was* true? He really has returned?

Orestes

Somewhat late. His treachery, on the other hand, 740
was promptness itself.

Pylades

What about that bitch Helen?
Did he bring her home?

Orestes

No, the other way around.
She brought him.

Pylades

Where is she hiding now?
Where is that woman who murdered so many Argives?

Orestes

In my house—if I have any right to call it mine.

Pylades

What did you ask Menelaus?

Orestes

To intercede for us   745
and save our lives.

Pylades

By god, what did he say to that?
This I want to hear.

Orestes

Oh, patience, caution, and so on.
The usual rot that traitors talk.

Pylades

But what was his excuse?
That tells me everything.

Orestes

We were interrupted.
That old man came. You know the man I mean—   750
the father of those precious daughters.

Pylades

Tyndareus himself?
Furious with you, I suppose, because of your mother?

Orestes

You've hit it. So Menelaus took the old man's side
against my father.

Pylades

He refused to help you at all?

Orestes

Oh, he's no soldier—though he's quite the man
with the ladies.

Pylades

As matters now stand, your death is certain?   755

Orestes

They vote on our sentence today.

Pylades
                                    I dread your answer,
  but what will their verdict be?

Orestes
                                    Life or death.
  Little words with large gestures.

Pylades
                                    Take Electra
  and try to make your escape.

Orestes
                                    No. Impossible.   760
  There are sentries posted everywhere.

Pylades
                                    I remember now.
  Armed men were patrolling the streets.

Orestes
                                    We are surrounded
  like a city under siege.

Pylades
                              Ask what happened to me.
  I have suffered too.

Orestes
                          Your troubles on top of mine?
  What happened?

Pylades
                    My father Strophius banished me from Phocis.   765

Orestes
  Banished you? On his authority as your father?
  Or did he take you to court on a formal indictment?

Pylades
  For aiding and abetting the murder of your mother—
  that "shocking crime," as he calls it.

Orestes

                              Heaven help me,
if you must suffer on my account!

Pylades

                              I am no Menelaus.
I can take it.

Orestes

                  But aren't you afraid of the Argives?   770
Suppose they decide to put you to death with me?

Pylades

    They have no jurisdiction. I am a Phocian.

Orestes

    Don't be too certain. In the hands of vicious men,
    a mob will do anything.

Pylades

                        But under good leaders
it's quite a different story.

Orestes

                    By god, that's *it!*
We must speak to them ourselves.

Pylades

                        But why should we?

Orestes

    Suppose, for instance, I went to the meeting myself   775
    and told them—

Pylades

                That you were completely justified?

Orestes

    That I avenged my father.

Pylades

                    They'd arrest you with pleasure.

Orestes

But what am I supposed to do? Sit here and sulk?
Die without saying a word in my own defense?

Pylades

A coward's act.

Orestes

Then, for god's sake, what *should* I do?

Pylades

Do you have anything to gain from staying here?

Orestes

Nothing whatsoever.

Pylades

And if you go to the meeting?

Orestes

Something might be gained.

Pylades

Then, clearly, you have to go. 780

Orestes

Good enough. I'll go.

Pylades

You may be killed, of course,
but at least you'll die fighting.

Orestes

And escape a coward's death.

Pylades

Better than by staying here.

Orestes

And my cause is just.

Pylades

Pray heaven that it seem that way to them.

Orestes

    Besides, they may pity me—

Pylades

                  Yes, your high birth.

Orestes

    Or they may feel indignation at my father's murder.   785

Pylades

    Then our course is clear.

Orestes

              Absolutely. I must go.
    I refuse to die a coward's death.

Pylades

              Spoken like a man.

Orestes

    Wait. Should we tell Electra?

Pylades

            Great heavens, no!

Orestes

    There'd probably be tears.

Pylades

            Which wouldn't be auspicious.

Orestes

    Clearly silence is best.

Pylades

          And will save no little time.

Orestes

    One strong objection still remains.

Pylades

              What's that?   790

Orestes

    My madness. If I have an attack—

Pylades

                              Have no fear.

You are in good hands.

Orestes

                       Madmen are hard to handle.

Pylades

  I will manage.

Orestes

              But if my madness strikes you too?

Pylades

  Forget it.

Orestes

          You're certain then? You're not afraid?

Pylades

  Afraid? Fear in friendship is an ugly trait.

Orestes

  Then lead on, helmsman.

Pylades

                Love leads you. Follow me.   795

Orestes

  Take me first to my father's grave.

Pylades

                     What for?

Orestes

  To implore his help.

Pylades

             Agreed. This pilgrimage is good.

Orestes

  But don't, for god's sake, let me see my mother's grave!

Pylades

No. She hated you.
                         But hurry. We must go now,
or the Argives may have voted before we arrive.
Here, lean yourself on me.
                              Now let the people jeer!   800
I'll lead you through the city, proud and unashamed.
What is my friendship worth unless I prove it now
in your time of trouble?

Orestes

                    "Provide yourself with friends
as well as kin," they say. And the proverb tells the truth.
One loyal friend is worth ten thousand relatives.   805

                         (*Exeunt Orestes and Pylades.*)

Chorus

Where, where are they now—
that glister of golden pride,
glory that camped at Troy
beside the Simois,
the boast of happiness
blazoned through Hellas?
Back and back they ebb,   810
a glory decays,
the greatness goes
from the happy house of Atreus.
Beneath the proud facade
the stain was old already—
strife for a golden ram,
and the long stain spread
as the curse of blood began—
slaughter of little princes,   815
a table laid with horror,
a feast of murdered sons.
And still corruption swelled,

murder displacing murder,
as through the blooded years
the stain spread on in time
to reach at last
the living heirs of Atreus.

And what had seemed so right,
as soon as done, became
evil, monstrous, wrong!
A mother murdered—
her soft throat slashed   820
by the stabbing sword,
and the blade raised high
while the brandished blood
fell warm from the steel,
staining, defiling
the sun's immaculate light.
Damnable, awful crime!
Sacrilege of madness born!
In horror, in anguish,
before she died,
his mother screamed—   825
No, no, my son, no!
Do not kill your mother
to revenge your father!
Do not make your life
an eternity of shame!   830

What madness like this?
What terror, what grief
can compare with this?
Hands, hands of a son,
stained with mother's blood!
Horror too inhuman
for mortal mind to bear.
The man who slew his mother
murdered and went mad.   835

Raving Furies stalk him down,
his rolling eyes are wild—
mad eyes that saw
his mother bare her breast   840
over her cloth of gold—
saw, and seeing, stabbed,
avenging his father
with his mother's murder!

(*Electra appears from the palace and is startled
to find Orestes gone.*)

Electra

But where is Orestes? For god's sake, women,
where did he go? Has he had another attack?   845

Coryphaeus

No, Electra. He went to the Argive meeting
to stand his trial and speak in his own defense.
Upon what happens there your life depends.

Electra

But *why*? And who persuaded him?

Coryphaeus

                    Pylades.
But I think I see a messenger on the way.   850
He can answer your question.

(*Enter Messenger, an old peasant.*)

Messenger

                    Lady Electra,
poor daughter of our old general Agamemnon,
I bring you bad news.

Electra

                    If your news is bad,   855
I hardly need to guess: we must die.
The sentence is death.

Messenger
                    Yes. The Argives have voted
that you and your brother must die today.

Electra
                              Death. . . .

But I expected no less. For a long time now
I dreaded in my heart that this would happen.   860
But what did they say? What were the arguments
that condemned us to death?
                              And how are we to die,
my brother and I? By being stoned to death   865
or by the sword?

Messenger
                    By strange coincidence, ma'am,
I'd just now come into town from the country,
thinking to get some news of how things stood
with you and Orestes. Your family, you see,
always took good care of me and, for my part,
I stood by your father to the very end.
I may be only a poor peasant, ma'am,
but when it comes to loyalty, I'm as good   870
as any man.
                    Well then, I saw a crowd
go streaming up to take their seats on the hill—
the same place where they say old Danaus
held the first public meeting in Argos
when Aegyptus stood his trial.
                              But anyhow,
seeing all that crowd, I went up and asked,
"What's happening here? Is there a war?   875
What's all this excitement for?"
                              "Look down,"
says someone. "Don't you see Orestes there?
He's on his way to stand trial for his life."
Then I saw a sight I never saw before,

and one whose likes I never hope to see
again:
      Orestes and Pylades together,   880
the one hunched down with sickness and despair,
the other sharing his troubles like a brother
and helping him along.
         In any case,
as soon as the seats were filled, a herald rose.
"Who wishes," he cried, "to speak to the question?   885
What is your wish? Should the matricide Orestes
live or die?"
      Then Talthybius got up—
the same man who fought with your father at Troy.
But he spoke like the toady he always was:
a two-faced speech, compliments for your father   890
in contrast to Orestes, cheap malicious stuff
puffed out with rolling phrases. And the gist?
Orestes' example was dangerous for parents.
But, needless to say, he was all smiles and sweetness
for Aegisthus' cronies.
      But that's your herald for you—   895
always jumping for the winning side, the friend
of any man with influence or power.
        After him
prince Diomedes spoke. It was his opinion
that you both should be banished, not killed,
since, by so doing, Argos would be guiltless   900
of your blood. The response, however, was mixed:
some applauded, others booed.
      The next speaker
was one of those cocky loudmouths, an Argive
but not from Argos—if you take my meaning—
anybody's man—for a price, of course—
sure of himself and reckless in his bluster,   905
but glib enough to take his hearers in.
He moved that Orestes and you should be stoned

to death, while Tyndareus sat cheering him on, 915
and even spoke to that effect.
                                 But at last
someone stood up to take the other side.
Nothing much to look at, but a real man;
not the sort one sees loafing in the market
or public places, ma'am, but a small farmer,
part of that class on which our country depends; 920
an honest, decent, and god-fearing man,
and anxious, in the name of common sense,
to say his bit.
                 Now in this man's opinion,
Orestes deserved a crown. What had he done,
after all, but avenge his father's murder
by killing a godless, worthless, adulterous woman? 925
A woman, what was more, who kept men from war,
kept them at home, tormented by the fear
that if they left, those who stayed behind
would seduce their wives and destroy their families
and homes.
            He seemed to convince the better sort, 930
but no one spoke.
                   Then Orestes rose.
"Men of Argos," he said, "it was for your sake
as much as for my father that I killed my mother.
But if you sanction this murder of husbands by wives, 935
you might as well go kill yourselves right now
or accept the domination of your women.
But you *will not*, you *must not*, do it.
As things now stand, my father's unfaithful wife
is dead. But if you vote that I must die, 940
then the precedent my act establishes
must fall, and you are all as good as dead,
since wives will have the courage of their crimes."
In short, a fine speech, and yet he failed;
while that cheap blabber, by playing to the mob,

induced them to pass a sentence of death.   945
Poor Orestes was barely able to persuade them
not to stone him to death, and then only
by promising that you and he would kill yourselves
today.
                    Pylades, in tears, is bringing him home   950
from the meeting, followed by a group of friends,
all weeping and mourning. Such is his return,
and a bitter sight it is.
                        So prepare the ropes,
bring out the sword, for you must die
and leave the light. Neither your high birth
nor Apollo in his shrine at Delphi helped. No,   955
Apollo has destroyed you both.

Coryphaeus
                        Poor wretched girl.
Look at her now, her head hung down,
dumb with grief, trembling on the verge of tears....

Electra
    O country of Pelasgia,
    let me lead the cry of mourning!   960
    With white nails I furrow my cheeks,
    beat my breast,
    each blow struck
    for the queen of the dead,
    goddess Persephone underground!
    Mourn, you Cyclopean earth!   965
    Shear your hair, you virgins,
    and raise the cry of pity,
    pity for us who die,
    heirs of the fighting men of Hellas!   970

    Down and down, my house.
    Pelops' line is ended,

the ancient happy house,
its envied greatness gone.
Envy and resentment
out of heaven struck.
Envy was the vote   975
the men of Argos took.

O generations of men,
fleeting race of suffering mankind,
look, look on your hopes!
Look at your lives,
all those happy hopes
cut down with failure and crossed with death.
See, in endless long parade,
the passing generations go,
changing places, changing lives.   980
The suffering remains.
Change and grief consume our little light.

O gods in heaven, take me,
lift me to heaven's middle air
where the great rock,
shattered from Olympus,
swings and floats on golden lines!
Lift me, take me there
and let me cry my grief to Tantalus,   985
founder of my house,
father of my fathers,
who saw the curse begin—
saw the wingèd race
as Pelops' swerving car
spurred along the sea,
Myrtilus hurled in murder down,   990
the body tossed
from the hurtling car
where the boiling surf
pounds and batters on Geraestos!

And saw the curse drive on
and the spreading stain of blood—
the sign appear   995
in Hermes' flocks,
a ram with golden fleece,
portending terror,
doom to Atreus, breeder of horses,   1000
the quarrel in the blood
that drove the golden sun awry,
forced the glistering car
westward through the sky
where lonely Dawn drives down
her solitary steed.
And Zeus, in horror of that crime,
changed the paths   1005
where the seven Pleiades turned and flared.
And still the spreading stain,
murder displacing murder,
betrayal and broken faith,
Thyestes' feast of horror
and the adulterous love
of Aërope of Crete.   1010
And now the curse comes home,
the inescapable taint,
finding fulfilment at last
in my brother and me!

Coryphaeus

And here your brother comes
under his sentence of death.
And with him comes Pylades,
most loyal of his friends,   1015
guiding like a brother
poor Orestes' stumbling steps.

(*Enter Orestes, supported by Pylades.*
Electra bursts into tears.)

Electra

　Orestes—
　　　　　O gods, to see you standing there,
　so close to death, the grave so near—
　O gods, I cannot bear it! To see you now
　for the last, last time.... No! No! No!　　　　　　　　　1020

Orestes

　Enough, Electra. No more of these womanish tears.
　Resign yourself. It is hard, I know,
　but we must accept our fate.

Electra

　　　　　　　　　　　How *can* I stop?　　　　　　　1025
　Look, look at this light, this gleaming air
　we shall never see again!

Orestes

　　　　　　　　　　No more, Electra.
　Isn't it enough that the Argives have killed me?
　Must you kill me too? For god's sake,
　no more tears.

Electra

　　　　　　　　　But you are so young,
　so young to die! You should live, Orestes! *Live!*　　　1030

Orestes.

　In god's name, stop it! These cries of yours
　will make me a coward.

Electra

　　　　　　　　　But to *die*, Orestes!
　Life is sweet, sweet! No one wants to die.

Orestes

　No, but we have no choice. Our time has come.　　　　　1035
　We merely have to choose the way in which we die:
　by the sword or the rope.

Electra
                Kill me yourself then,
Orestes. Don't let some Argive disgrace
the daughter of Agamemnon.

Orestes
                   I have my mother's blood
upon my hands. I will not have yours too.   1040
Do it in any way you wish, but you must do it
yourself.

Electra
        If I must, then I must. But, Orestes,
don't die before I do! Please. O gods,
let me hold you. . . .

Orestes
            What is it worth,
this poor hollow pleasure—if those who die
have any pleasure left?

Electra
            Oh, my brother,
dearest, sweetest name I know—my life—   1045

Orestes
    O gods, this breaks my heart—
                  With all my love
I hold you in my arms.
               What shame on earth
can touch me any more?
              Oh, my sister,
these loving words, this last sweet embrace
is all that we shall ever know in life   1050
of marriage and children!

Electra
          If only one sword
could kill us both! If we could only share
one coffin together—

Orestes

Then death might be sweet.
But how little now of all our family is left   1055
to bury us.

Electra

Menelaus did nothing at all?
He betrayed our father like the coward he is?

Orestes

No, not once did he so much as show his face.
Not once. His eyes were glued upon the throne;
oh, he was careful not to help.
But come,
we must die as we were born—well,   1060
as the children and heirs of Agamemnon should.
I shall show the city of what blood I come
by falling on my sword. As for you,
follow my example and die bravely.
Pylades,
be the umpire of our deaths; then lay us out   1065
when we are dead, and make us both one grave
beside my father's tomb.
And now, goodbye.
I go to do what must be done.

Pylades

Wait!
Stop, Orestes. I have one reproach to make.
How could you think that I would want to live   1070
once you were dead?

Orestes

Why should my dying
mean that you should die?

Pylades

You can ask me that?
How can I live when my only friend is dead?

Orestes

It was I who murdered my mother, not you.

Pylades

We murdered together, and it is only just
that I share the cost with you.

Orestes

No,   1075

Pylades. Live; go home to your father.
You still have a country you can call your own;
I do not. You have your father's house
and you inherit wealth, great wealth.
That marriage with Electra which, as my friend,
I promised you, has failed. But marry elsewhere;   1080
have children.
                   The bonds which bound us once
are broken now. And now goodbye, my friend,
my best, my only friend.
                   And good luck.
Luck at least is something you may have,
but I cannot. The dead have lost their luck.

Pylades

How little you seem to understand, Orestes.   1085
If I desert you now to save myself,
may this green and growing earth refuse
my ashes, this golden air shelter me no more!
I murdered with you, and I affirm it
proudly. And it was I who planned that crime   1090
for which you suffer now, and I should die
with you and her.
                   Yes, with her, I said.
She is my wife, the wife you promised me.
What would my story be when I go home
to Delphi and Phocis?

Pylades bring issues toward P reminds Orestes of friendship etc.

That when all was well,   1095
I was your firm friend, but my friendship withered
when your luck ran out?

                    No, Orestes,
I have my duty too.

                    But since we have to die,
let us think and see if there is any way
of making Menelaus suffer too.

Orestes

Let me see that sight and I could die   1100
content.

Pylades

          Then do what I ask you and wait now.

Orestes

With pleasure, if only I can be revenged.

Pylades

               (*Drawing Orestes back out of hearing of the Chorus.*)
Whisper. Those women there—I don't trust them.

Orestes

They're all right. They're friends.

Pylades

                    Then listen.
We'll murder Helen. That will touch   1105
Menelaus where it hurts.

Orestes

          But how?
If we can manage it, I'm more than willing.

Pylades

A sword in the throat. Unless I'm mistaken,
she's hiding in your house now.

Orestes

Oh yes,
and putting her seals on everything we own.

Pylades

But not for long. Hades wants her, I think.

Orestes

But how can we do it? She has a retinue   1110
of slaves.

Pylades

Slaves? Is that all she has?
I'm not afraid of any Trojan slaves.

Orestes

Creatures who manage her perfume and mirrors!

Pylades

Gods! Did she bring those Trojan gewgaws home?

Orestes

Oh, Hellas is far too small to hold that woman now.

Pylades

What are slaves worth in a fight with men   1115
who were born free?

Orestes

If we can bring this off,
I'll gladly die twice.

Pylades

And so would I,
to get revenge for you.

Orestes

But describe your plan.
Every step.

Pylades
> First of all, we go inside
on the pretext of killing ourselves.

Orestes
> > Good enough. 1120
> But then?

Pylades
> Then we make a great show of tears
and tell her how much we suffer.

Orestes
> > At which, of course,
she'll burst into tears. But she'll be laughing inside.

Pylades
> Why then, so will we—exactly the same.

Orestes
> But how do we kill her?

Pylades
> > We'll carry swords 1125
> hidden in our robes.

Orestes
> > But what about her slaves?
We must kill them first.

Pylades
> > No, we'll lock them up
in different rooms.

Orestes
> > But if they scream for help,
then we'll kill them.

Pylades
> > And once we're through with them,
the way is clear. Right?

Orestes

                Death to Helen!   1130

That will be our motto.

Pylades

                Now you have it.

But observe the beauty of my plan.

                    First,

if we killed a better woman than Helen,

it would be plain murder.

                This is not.

No, we punish her in the name of all Hellas

whose fathers and sons she murdered, whose wives   1135

she widowed.

          Mark my words, Orestes.

There will be bonfires and celebrations in Argos;

men will call down blessings on our heads,

thank us, congratulate us for doing away

with a vicious, worthless woman. No longer   1140

shall they call you "the man who murdered his mother."

No, a fairer title awaits you now,

the better name of "the killer of Helen

who killed so many men."

                And why, in god's name,

should Menelaus prosper when you, your sister,

and your father have to die?—I omit your mother   1145

with good reason. If, through Agamemnon,

Menelaus has his wife, he *shall* not, *must* not,

have your house.

          For my part, let me die

if I do not lift my sword against that woman!

But should we fail, should she escape our hands,

we'll burn this house around us as we die!   1150

One way or another, Orestes, we shall not be cheated

of glory.

         Honor is ours if we die;

fame, if we escape.

Coryphaeus

Every woman
loathes and despises the name of Helen, the woman
who disgraced her sex.

Orestes

Nothing in this world   1155
is better than a friend. For one good friend
I would not take in trade either power or money
or all the people of Argos. It was you,
my best friend, who planned our murder of Aegisthus.
You shared the risks with me, and once again,
good friend, you give me my revenge   1160
and all your help.

But I say no more,
lest I embarrass you by praising you
so much.

I have to die. Very well then,
but above all else I want my death
to hurt the man I hate. He betrayed me,   1165
he made me suffer, so let him suffer now
for what he did to me.

Am I or am I not
the son of Agamemnon, the man who ruled all Hellas,
not as a tyrant, but almost as a god,
with godlike power?

And I shall not shame him
by dying like a slave. No, I die free,
and I shall have my free revenge on you,   1170
Menelaus!

That revenge alone
would make me happy. If—which I doubt—
we could murder Helen and then escape,
so much the better. But this is a dream,
a prayer, a futile hope. It cheers the heart,   1175
but nothing more.

Electra
                    Orestes, I have the answer!
  A way out for us all!

Orestes
                    That would take a god.
  But go ahead, Electra. I know your shrewdness   1180
  of mind.

Electra
              Listen then. You too, Pylades.
Orestes
  Go on. Good news would make pleasant hearing now.

Electra
  Do you remember Helen's daughter, Hermione?

Orestes
  That little girl our mother took care of?

Electra
                                        Yes.
  She has gone now to Clytemnestra's tomb.   1185

Orestes
  What for? And what if she has?

Electra
                              She went
  to pour libations on our mother's grave.
Orestes
                              And so?
  What does this have to do with our escape?

Electra
  Seize her as a hostage when she comes back.

Orestes
  What good will that do?

Electra
Listen, Orestes.   1190

Once Helen is dead, Menelaus may attempt
to hurt one of us three—you or him or me—
though it hardly matters who: we are all one here.
Well, let him try. You merely set your sword
at Hermione's throat and warn him you will kill her
at the first false move. If then, seeing Helen   1195
lying in a pool of blood, he decides he wants
his daughter's life at least and agrees to spare you,
let the girl go. On the other hand,
if he tries to kill you in a frantic burst of rage,
you slit the girl's throat. He may bluster   1200
in the beginning, but he'll soon see reason,
I think. The man's a coward, as you know:
he won't fight.
And there you have my plan
for making our escape.

Orestes
What a woman!
The mind of a man with a woman's loveliness!   1205
If ever a woman deserved to live, not die,
that woman is you.
What do you say now,
Pylades? Will you forfeit a woman like this
by dying, or will you live, marry her,
and be happy?

Pylades
Nothing would please me more.
My dearest wish is to go home to Phocis
with Electra as my bride.

Orestes
Electra, I like your plan   1210
in every respect—provided we can catch
the traitor's cub. How soon, do you think,
will Hermione return?

Electra

Any moment now.
The time at least is exactly right.

Orestes

Perfect.   1215
Electra, you stay here outside the house
and wait for her. Make certain that no one,
and especially no friend of her father,
slips into the house. But if someone does,   1220
beat with your fist on the door or raise a cry,
but let us know.

You and I, Pylades—
I know I can count on your help now, my friend—
will go inside, get our swords and make ready
to settle our score with Helen.

(He raises his arms in prayer and invokes
the ghost of Agamemnon.)

O my father,   1225
ghost who walks the house of blackest night,
your son Orestes calls upon your help
in his hour of need! It is for you, Father,
I suffer. For you I was condemned to death
unjustly! And your own brother has betrayed me,
though what I did was right. Come, Father,
help me to capture his wife! Help me kill her!   1230
O Father, help us now!

Electra

O my father,
if you can hear our prayers beneath the earth,
come, rise in answer! We die for you!

Pylades

O Agamemnon, kinsman of my father,
hear my prayers!
Help us! Save your children!

Orestes

I murdered my mother!

Pylades

                     I held the sword that killed!   1235

Electra

I encouraged them! I made them brave!

Pylades

Hear our reproaches and save your children now!

Orestes

I offer my tears to you—

Electra

                  And I my grief.

Pylades

Enough.
          We must be about our business now.   1240
If prayers can penetrate this earth below,
he hears.
       —O Zeus, Zeus of our fathers,
great power of justice, help us now,
help us to victory!
             Three friends together,
one common cause, one right,
and together we shall live or die!   1245

                 (Orestes and Pylades enter the palace.)

Electra

Women of Mycenae, noble women of Argos,
a word with you, please.

Coryphaeus

             What is it, my lady?
For you are mistress still in the city of Argos.   1250

Electra

I want half of you to watch the highway.
The rest of you will stand guard over here.

Coryphaeus

But why, lady?

Electra

          A premonition. I am afraid   1255
there may be murderers lurking about the house.
Fresh blood may be spilt.

      *(The Chorus divides into two sections, each section led by a
          Parastate, and goes to opposite sides of the orchestra.)*

First Parastate

              To your posts, women!
I'll watch the road to the east.

Second Parastate

             And I'll watch here   1260
on the westward side.

Electra

         Keep a close lookout
on both sides now. Look all around you.

Coryphaeus

We obey.

Electra

       Stay alert now. Look sharp.   1265

First Parastate

Someone is coming! Look—a peasant
approaching the palace.

Electra

          Then this is the end.   1270
He'll betray our ambush to our enemies.

First Parastate

No. A false alarm. The road is empty.
There's no one there.

Electra

You on the other side,
is all well? Is there anyone in sight?   1275

Second Parastate

All's well here. You watch there.
Not an Argive in sight anywhere here.

First Parastate

Nor here either. Not a soul in sight.   1280

Electra

Wait then. I'll go and call in at the door.

(She goes to the palace and calls inside.)

Why are you so quiet?
Why this delay?
For god's sake, kill her!
They don't answer.   1285
Not a sound. O gods, what has happened?
Has her loveliness blunted their swords?
In a few minutes the soldiers will be here
to rescue her, rushing up with drawn swords!   1290
Back to your posts.
Look sharper than ever.
This is no time for napping.

Coryphaeus

I'm watching.   1295

Helen (from within)

Help me, Argos! Help! They'll murder me!

First Parastate

Did you hear her scream? They're killing her!

Second Parastate

That awful cry! That was Helen screaming!

Electra

O Zeus, Zeus, send us strength!
Come, O Zeus! Help them now!   1300

Helen (*from within*)

Help me, Menelaus! Help! I'm dying—

Electra

Murder!

        Butcher!

             Kill!

Thrust your twin swords home!
Slash, now slash again!
Run the traitress through,
kill the whore who killed   1305
so many brave young men—
the wounded and the dead,
those for whom we mourn,
those murdered and dying
where the waters of Scamander
eddy and roar!   1310

Coryphaeus

Wait, Electra.

            I hear the sound of footsteps.
Someone is coming.

Electra

           It must be Hermione.
Yes, it is! It is! Hermione herself,
at the very moment of murder.

               But not a sound.
Look at her—walking straight for our trap,   1315
and a sweet catch she is, if I can take her.
Quick, back to your posts.

Seem natural
and unconcerned; don't give us away.
I had better have a sullen sort of look,
as though nothing had happened here.   1320

                        (*Enter Hermione.*)
                       Ah,
have you been to Clytemnestra's grave, dear?
Did you wreathe it with flowers and pour libations?

Hermione

Yes, I gave her all the dues of the dead.
But, you know, I was frightened coming home.
I thought I heard a scream in the distance.   1325

Electra

                       A cry?
Really? But surely we have every right
to cry a little.

Hermione

            Not *more* trouble, Electra?
What has happened now?

Electra

              Orestes and I
have been sentenced to death.

Hermione

               God forbid!
You, my own cousins, must die?

Electra

               We must.
This is necessity whose yoke we bear.   1330

Hermione

Then that was why I heard that cry?

Electra

                  Yes.
He went and fell at Helen's knees—

Hermione

Who went?
I don't understand.

Electra

Orestes. To implore Helen
to save our lives.

Hermione

Then well might the palace   1335
have rung with your cries.

Electra

What better reason
could there be?
But if you love us, dear,
go now, fall at your mother's feet
and beg her, implore her by her happiness
to intercede with Menelaus now
on our behalf. My mother nursed you in her arms: 1340
have pity on us now and save our lives.
Go plead with her. You are our last hope.
I will take you there myself.

Hermione

Oh yes, yes!
I must go quickly! If it lies in my power,   1345
you are saved.

(Exit Hermione into the palace. Electra
follows her to the door.)

Electra

For god's sake, Orestes,
Pylades! Lift your swords and seize your prey!

Hermione (from within)

Who are these men?
Help!
Save me!

Orestes *(from within)*
                                        Silence,
    girl.
        You are here to save us, not yourself.

Electra
    Hold her, seize her!
                        Put your sword to her throat   1350
    and stop her screaming.
                        Let Menelaus learn
    with whom he has to deal now. Show him
    what it means to fight with men, not cowards
    from Troy. Make him suffer for his crimes!

        (Electra enters the palace, closing the great doors behind her.
                From the palace comes the sound of commotion,
                        scuffling, cries, and muffled screams.)

Chorus

    —Quick, raise a shout!

    —   A cry!

    —Drown the sound of murder in the palace!

    —A shout, before the Argives hear   1355
        and come running to the rescue!

    —Before they come, first let me see
        dead Helen, lying in her blood,
        or hear the story from her slaves.

Coryphaeus
    Some horror has happened; but what I do not know.   1360

Chorus
    —God's vengeance on Helen,
        justice crashing from heaven!

—Justice for Helen
  who made all Hellas mourn,
  mourn for her lover's sake—

—For Paris, bitter curse of Ida,   1365
  Paris, who led all Hellas to Troy!

Coryphaeus
  Hush. Be still.
              The bolts on the great doors
are sliding—someone is coming out—
some slave who can tell us what has happened.

           (Breathless and incoherent with terror, a Phrygian
                    slave bursts from the palace.)

Phrygian
  Greekish sword—kill dead!
  Trojan scared, oh.
               Run, run,
  jump in slippers, fast, fast,   1370
  clop-clop clamber over roof.
  Hole in beams, inside court,
  jump down
          boom!
             below.
  Oh, oh.
          Where can run, where go?   1375
  Mebbe foreign ladies know?
              Up, up,
  soar in air, him shimmer nothing?
  Swim in sea—mebbe? mebbe?—
  where godbull ocean cradles world
  flowing water with?

Coryphaeus
  In god's name, speak, servant of Helen!   1380

Phrygian

Oh, oh,

      Ilium, Ilium, Troy, Troy!

Holy hill of Ida, green one, O growing!

Ai ai,

      Ilium, Troy,

hear the dirge I cry,

          ai ai, 1385

death by Helenbeauty brought,

eye of doom,

of birdborn loveliness the eye,

lovely eye of swan of Zeus,

swan that sank in Leda's lap,

eye of passion, glancing death,

eye of love

that broke the burnished walls of Troy! 1390

Pity, pity, I cry

for Ganymede of Troy,

         ai ai,

ravished to bed

by Zeus the rider!

Coryphaeus

Tell us what happened as clearly as you can.

Phrygian

Ailinos! 1395

     Ailinos!

Ailinos! the dirge begins,

the dirge we cry

for royal blood and princes dead

by sword, by sword!

      Ai ai!

But ladies, I tell you all

and how come happen.

Into palace came   1400
a pride of lions, Greekers, twins.
One of general Agamemnon, son;
other Pylades, man of plots, evil, *bad;*
Odysseus kind of, bluffer, cheater,
loyal, yes, and bold, bold,   1405
skills for war, of killer-snake.
God darn him dead
for plotty sneaks,
                    I hope.
But walk they in. Tears, tears.
Sobs for Helen Pariswife.   1410
Oh so humble, sit 'em down,
one on left, one on right.
But swords too!
                And then—*well!*
Put their hands on lady's *knee,*
begging life.
                Slaves are scared.   1415
Terror, terror, skitter, scatter.
One man say, "Hey, treachery!"
"Look out, lady!" someone cry.
No no no guess other slaves,
but some are thinking,
                        "Hey,   1420
snake who killed his mother
lady Helen tangled has
in webbery of plot."

Coryphaeus

And where were you? Or had you run away?   1425

Phrygian

No, no, no.
                In Eastern way   1430
with foreign fan of feathers, yes,

fan the hair of lady Helen,
rippling air, to and fro,
gently over cheeks of ma'am.
And while I fan,
                    slow, slow,
Helen's fingers wind the flax.
Spindle turning, fingers moving,
round and round the flax on floor,
Trojan spoils for cloth of purple,   1435
gift, yes, for sister's tomb.
Oh, oh.
          Orestes speaks:
"Deign, O ma'am, child of Zeus,
down from dais, please to step.
Stand by ancient Pelops' altar,   1440
hear my talk, but private, please."
So he led her, lady go,
poor suspecting nothing Helen.
Meanwhile, yes, evil friend,
partner Pylades of crime,   1445
is doing work.
              "Go, go!" he shout,
"Trojan cowards, slaves, slaves!"
Oh, and then he lock them up,
some in stables, others rooms,
here, there,
          oh oh,
from lady Helen barred away!   1450

Coryphaeus
    And then what happened? Go on.

Phrygian
        Oh! Oh! Oh!
                O Mother Ida!
    Horror, horror, oh, and crime!

What I saw in house of princes!
Never, never.

        Out of hiding,   1455
out of purply cloaks
they drew their swords!
And eyes of them! Oh, going round
to see if danger anywhere.   1460
And then they came.

        Oh, boars
they were, yes, boars attacking,
screaming, shouting,

           "Die! Die!
Die for traitor husband, coward
who betrayed his brother's son,
who left him to die in Argos!"
Lady screamed,

        ah, ah,   1465
snow-white arms, flailing, flailing,
beating bosom, beating breast!
Hair she tore, in sandals goldy
leaped to run!

        But after, after,
came Orestes

        Caught her, oh,   1470
winding fingers in her hair
and neck forced back,

        down, down,
against her shoulder
Lifted, ah, sword to strike—

Coryphaeus

   But where were her servants? Couldn't you help?

Phrygian

   Oh, we shout, yes!

        We batter doors

with iron bars, break down panels   1475
where we are!
                Then run, run,
rescue, rescue! Some with stones,
with swords, with spears.
                     But *then!*
Pylades came on—ooh, brave!
Hectorlike or Ajax with his helms of triple   1480
(I saw him once in Priampalace).
Steel on steel together meet,
but soon we see
Trojan men no match for Greek.   1485
Ai ai,
          one run, one dead,
wounded this and begging that.
So quick, quick, run, hide!
Falling some, dying others,
staggering is one with wounds.
And then, oh!
                Hermione came in   1490
as mother Helen sank to die.
Men stop, yes, Bacchantes,
dropping wands for seizing prey,
snatch at girl, then turn back
to kill, kill madam dead.   1495
But then, oh then—
suddenly, ah, ah!
madam vanish,
fly through roof
as though some magic mebbe mebbe
or robbery of thiever gods!
O Earth! O Zeus! O Night!
What then happen I not know.
No, no, run, I ran!
But Menelaus, *ai*—
all his suffer, all his hurt   1500

to bring the lady Helen home,
ah ah,
        nothing is.

Coryphaeus

  On and on it goes, strangeness to strangeness
  succeeding, horror to horror.
                              And look—
  here Orestes comes rushing from the palace   1505
  with drawn sword!

                    (*Enters Orestes in haste, his sword drawn.*)

Orestes
                    Where is that coward slave
  who ran from my sword inside?

Phrygian
                              I bow down, yessir.
  I kiss the ground, lord. Is Eastern custom, yes.

Orestes

  This is Argos, fool, not Troy.

Phrygian
                              But anywhere
  wise man wants to live, not die.

Orestes
                              And those screams of yours?
  Admit it: you were shouting to Menelaus for help.   1510

Phrygian

  Oh no, nosir. Not I. For you I was screaming.
  You needed help.

Orestes
                    Did Helen deserve to die?

Phrygian

  Oh, yessir. Three times cut madam's throat,
  and I not object.

Orestes

This is cowardly flattery.
You don't believe it.

Phrygian

Oh sir, I believe, sure.
Helen ruin Hellas, yes, kill Trojans too. 1515

Orestes

Swear you're telling me the truth or I'll kill you.

Phrygian

Oh, oh! By life I swear—if life can have mebbe?

Orestes

(*Lowering his sword still closer to the Phrygian's throat.*)
Were all the Trojans as terrified by cold steel
as you?

Phrygian

Ooh, please, please, not so close!
All shiny bloody!

Orestes

What are you afraid of, fool?
Is it some Gorgon's head to turn you into stone? 1520

Phrygian

Not stone, corpse yes. But this Gorgon thing
I do not know.

Orestes

What? Nothing but a slave
and afraid to die? Death might end your suffering.

Phrygian

Slave man, free man, everybody like to live.

Orestes

Well spoken. Your wit saves you. Now get inside.

Phrygian

You will not kill me?

Orestes

I spare you.

Phrygian

Oh, thank you, thank you.   1525

Orestes

Go, or I'll change my mind.

Phrygian

I no thank you for that.

(Exit Phrygian.)

Orestes

Fool, did you think I'd dirty my sword on your neck?
Neither man nor woman—who could want your life?
No, I came to stop your frightened screams. This city
of Argos is quickly roused to arms by any cry   1530
for help.
          Not that I'm afraid of Menelaus either.
No, let him come. His glory is his golden curls,
not his sword.
          But if he brings the Argives here
and in revenge for Helen's death refuses his help
to my sister, my friend and helper, or myself,   1535
then his daughter too shall join his wife in death.

(Exit Orestes into palace, bolting the doors behind him.)

Chorus

O gods! Murder!
Grief comes down once more
upon the house of Atreus!

First Parastate

What should we do? Send to the city for help,
or keep silent?

Second Parastate

Silence is the safer course.   1540

(*A lurid red glare suffused with billowing smoke
suddenly lights up the roof of the palace.*)

First Parastate

Look! Look up there on the roof—the smoke
pouring, billowing up!

Second Parastate

And the glare of torches!
They are burning the house, the ancestral house!
They shrink from nothing, not even murder!

Chorus

—God works his way with man.   1545

—The end is as god wills.

—Great is the power of god.

—And great it has been here

—where the fiend of vengeance drives,

—blood for blood, against this house,

—in vengeance for Myrtilus!

Coryphaeus

Wait. I see Menelaus coming this way
in great haste. He must have heard some news
of what has happened here.
                        Stand your guard,   1550
inside the house! Quick, bolt the palace doors.
Beware, Orestes.
                This man in his hour of triumph
is dangerous. Take care.

(Enter Menelaus with armed attendants.)

Menelaus

I have come
to investigate a tale of incredible crimes   1555
committed by two lions—I cannot bring myself
to call them men.

I am also told that Helen
is not dead, but has disappeared, vanished
into thin air, the idiotic fiction
of a man whose mind was almost crazed with fear
or, more probably, as I suspect, the invention
of the matricide and patently absurd.   1560
Inside there, open the doors!

(Dead silence.)

Very well.
Men, break down that door so I can rescue
my poor daughter from the hands of these murderers
and recover Helen's body.

In revenge for her,   1565
I personally shall put these men to death.

*(Dimly visible in the swirling smoke, Orestes and Pylades appear
on the roof, with Hermione between them. Orestes holds
a sword at Hermione's throat. Farther back stands
Electra with torches blazing.)*

Orestes

You there, don't lay a finger on that door.
Yes, I mean you, Menelaus, you braggart!
Touch that door and I'll rip the parapet
from this crumbling masonry and smash your skull.   1570
The doors have been bolted down with iron bars
on purpose to keep you out.

Menelaus

Gods in heaven!
Torches blazing—and people standing on the roof

like a city under siege, and—*no!*
A man holding a sword at my daughter's throat!   1575

Orestes

   Do you want me to ask the questions, Menelaus,
   or would you prefer that I do the talking?

Menelaus

                       Neither.
   But I suppose I must listen.

Orestes

             For your information,
   I am about to kill your daughter.

Menelaus

               Her too?
   Wasn't it enough that you murdered her mother?

Orestes

   No, heaven stole her and robbed me of the pleasure.   1580

Menelaus

   This is mockery. Do you deny you killed her?

Orestes

   It pains me to deny it. Would to god I had!

Menelaus

   Had what? This suspense is torture.

Orestes

                 Killed her.
   Struck down the whore who pollutes our land.

Menelaus

   Let me have her body. Let me bury her.   1585

Orestes

Ask the gods for her carcass. In the meanwhile
I will kill your daughter.

Menelaus

                           The mother-killer
murders again!

Orestes

                    His father's avenger
and betrayed by you.

Menelaus

                           Wasn't her death enough?

Orestes

I can never have my fill of killing whores.   1590

Menelaus

But you, Pylades! Are you his partner
in this murder too?

Orestes

                    His silence says he is.
But I speak for him.

Menelaus

                    If I catch you,
you will regret this act.

Orestes

                    We won't run away.
In fact, we'll burn the house.

Menelaus

                           Burn the house!   1595
Burn the palace of your fathers?

Orestes

                           To keep it from you.
But your daughter dies. First the sword,
then the fire.

Menelaus

        Kill her. I shall get revenge.

Orestes

  Very well.

Menelaus

       No, wait! *For god's sake, no!*

Orestes

  Silence. You suffer justly for what you did.

Menelaus

  Can justice let you live?

Orestes

           Live—and reign too!   1600

Menelaus

  Reign where?

Orestes

      Here in Argos.

Menelaus

         You?

  You officiate as priest?

Orestes

        And why not?

Menelaus

  Or sacrifice for war?

Orestes

       If you can, I can too.

Menelaus

  My hands are clean.

Orestes

       Your hands, yes, but not your heart.

Menelaus

  Who would speak to you?

Orestes
Those who love their fathers.   1605

Menelaus
And those who love their mothers?

Orestes
Were born lucky.

Menelaus
That leaves you out.

Orestes
Yes. I loathe whores.

Menelaus
Then keep that sword away from her!

Orestes
Guess again,
traitor.

Menelaus
Could you kill my child?

Orestes
Ah, the truth
at last!

Menelaus
What do you want?

Orestes
Persuade the people —   1610

Menelaus
Persuade them of what?

Orestes
To let us live.

Menelaus
Or you will kill my child?

Orestes
It comes to that.

Menelaus
  O gods, my poor wife—

Orestes
                  No pity for me?

Menelaus
  —brought home to die!

Orestes
               Would to god she had!

Menelaus
  All my countless labors—

Orestes
              Nothing done for me.   1615

Menelaus
  All I suffered—

Orestes
        Is irrelevant to me.

Menelaus
  I am trapped.

Orestes
       Trapped by your own viciousness.
All right, Electra, set the house on fire!
You there, Pylades, most loyal of my friends,
burn the roof! Set those parapets   1620
to blazing!

Menelaus
      Help, help, people of Danaus,
knights of Argos!
        To arms! To arms!
This man with mother's blood upon his hands
threatens our city, our very lives!

(General alarm. Suddenly Apollo appears ex machina *above the palace. Behind him on the same level stands Helen.)*

Apollo
                                        Stop,   1625
Menelaus. Calm your anger.
                        It is I,
a god, Phoebus Apollo, son of Leto,
who speak.
                You too, Orestes, standing there
with drawn sword over that girl, hear
what I say.
                Helen is here with me—
yes, that same Helen whom you tried to kill   1630
out of hatred for Menelaus. This is she
whom you see enfolded in the gleaming air,
delivered from death. You did not kill her.
For I, so commanded by Zeus the father,
snatched her from your sword.
                                Helen lives,
for being born of Zeus, she could not die,   1635
and now, between the Dioscuri in the swathe
of air, she sits enthroned forever, a star
for sailors.
                Menelaus must marry again,
since the gods by means of Helen's loveliness
drove Trojans and Greeks together in war   1640
and made them die, that earth might be lightened
of her heavy burden of mortality.
So much for Helen.
                        I now turn to you,
Orestes.
                It is your destiny to leave this land
and go in exile to Parrhasia for a year.   1645
Henceforth that region shall be named for you,
called Oresteion by the Arcadians and Azanians.
From there you must go to the city of Athena

and render justice for your mother's murder
to the three Eumenides.

          Gods shall be your judges,   1650
sitting in holy session on the hill of Ares,
and acquitting you by sacred verdict.
                     Then,
Orestes, you shall marry Hermione,
the girl against whose throat your sword now lies.
Neoptolemus hopes to make her his wife,   1655
but never shall, for he is doomed to die
when he comes to Delphi seeking justice
for his father's death.
              Give Electra in marriage
to Pylades as you promised. Great happiness
awaits him.
         Let Orestes reign in Argos,   1660
Menelaus. But go yourself and be king in Sparta,
the dowry of Helen, whose only dowry yet
has been your anguish and suffering.
                  I myself
shall reconcile the city of Argos to Orestes,
for it was I who commanded his mother's murder.   1665
I compelled him to kill.

Orestes

           Hail, Apollo,
for your prophetic oracles! True prophet,
not false!
          And yet, when I heard you speak,
I thought I heard the whispers of some fiend
speaking through your mouth.
                But all is well,   1670
and I obey.
          See, I now release Hermione,
and we shall marry if her father gives
his blessing and consent.

Menelaus

Farewell, Helen,
daughter of Zeus! I envy you your home
and happiness among the gods.

Orestes,   1675
I now betroth my only child to you,
as Apollo commands.

We come of noble birth
and nobly may this marriage bless us both.

Apollo

Let each one go to his appointed place.
Now let your quarrels end.

Menelaus

I obey, lord.

Orestes

And I. Menelaus, I accept our truce   1680
and make my peace with Apollo and his oracle.

Apollo

Let each one go his way.
Go and honor Peace,
loveliest of goddesses.
Helen I now lead
to the halls of Zeus,
upon the road that turns
among the blazing stars.   1685
There with Hera she shall sit,
with Heracles and Hebe throned,
a goddess forever,
forever adored—
there between her brothers,
the sons of Zeus,
reigning on the seas,
a light to sailors.   1690

(Exeunt Menelaus and retinue, Orestes arm in arm
with Hermione, Pylades and Electra,
as the Chorus files out.)

Chorus

Hail, O Victory!
Preserve my life
and let me wear the crown!

IPHIGENIA IN AULIS

Translated by Charles R. Walker

INTRODUCTION TO
IPHIGENIA IN AULIS

THE *Iphigenia in Aulis* was produced, together with the *Bacchae* and the *Alcmaeon*, at the Great Dionysia in March, 405 B.C., a few months after Euripides' death. It seems probable that Euripides' son (some say his nephew) produced the play and perhaps filled in parts of the script which Euripides had left incomplete at the time of his death.

The play is full of invention and dramatic reversals. Some classical critics, dubbing it pure melodrama, have felt that it represented a woeful falling-off from the sterner standards of Greek tragedy. Most students of dramatic literature find it an exciting "transition piece," for it is an obvious bridge between classical tragedy and postclassical drama. But whatever else it may be, for the majority of readers, both scholarly and other, it is still tragic, still Greek, and still Euripides.

Euripides here, more than ever, takes liberties with his legendary material. The legend briefly is this: Iphigenia, daughter of Agamemnon, is sacrificed to the goddess Artemis, to persuade her to grant the Greek ships a favoring wind on their way to conquer Troy. But the great heroes of Homer are cut down to size, or below, to human, almost modern, politicians preparing to fight a war out of ambition or fear. In Homer, Agamemnon, "king of men," while not as glamorous a hero as Hector or Odysseus, is nevertheless a man of courage, a first-rate commander, a king. In the *Iphigenia* he has become an ambitious politician, wavering in his motives, and a moral, if not a physical, coward. Menelaus is also of doubtful character. Achilles, to be sure, has something of the hero about him, but it is the heroism of a very human youth, not of an adult Homeric warrior. As to Iphigenia, her character has been transformed from an unwilling victim into a true saint. She does not appear in Homer, but tradition pictures Iphigenia as a gagged, unwilling victim, appealing with her eyes, even at the moment of her death, for pity. This, for example, is the Iphigenia of Aeschylus' *Agamemnon*. Euripides remolds her character and so the plot he derives from the legend. In this play, she gives her life (much as Joan of Arc did) in accordance with what she regards as the "divine will" and the needs of her country.

I have suggested that the play is more modern than most Greek tragedies; perhaps it is more modern than any of them. But in what sense is it modern? First of all in techniques of the theater: it is full of new dramatic devices as well as a concentration of old ones. Instead of the formal Euripidean prologue giving the audience background for the plot, there is a lively duologue full of dramatic tension between Agamemnon and a servant. (An old-style prologue also exists and in this version is integrated into the dialogue, ll. 49-114.) The chorus is no longer essential to the dramatic action but it often establishes the mood. It consists in this play of women who have crossed over from their native Chalcis to Aulis, apparently as sightseers to see the heroes and the famous Greek fleet. Their vivid description of the army and the ships in the first chorus seems comparable in function to scenery in the modern theater or to background shots in a motion picture. Part of the role of the normal chorus appears to have been taken over by an increase in the number and significance of solos, or arias. As to the plot, it is tight; the action, rapid and full of surprises. Aristotle found Iphigenia's quick change in attitude toward her destiny hard to believe. Most modern readers, or hearers of the play, do not. Finally, in several scenes there are intimate conversations and expressions of what we would call "sentiment."

The text of *Iphigenia* is unusually corrupt, and there is by no means agreement among scholars as to what should be attributed to Euripides and what to later interpolators. But on many strategic passages there is general agreement. In this connection the present translator had a revealing experience. Being thoroughly familiar with the play but only slightly familiar with the conclusions of textual commentators, he prepared an acting version in English for the modern stage. This necessitated some cutting from choruses and dialogue of passages which to him seemed padded, irrelevant, or undramatic. In comparing the acting version with what the textual commentators had been saying, he found that he had dropped most of the spurious passages. In short, it is here suggested that there has come to us *from the hand of Euripides* a highly playable script. This translation, it should be said, is based on the *whole* text. The spurious ending, or exodus, together with a few lines omitted as either spurious or interfering with the dramatic tension, is given in the Appendix.

Here, then, we have a play which in action, mood of disillusioned realism, number of heroic characters "debunked," and in intimate, even domestic, dialogue appears very modern indeed. And yet, the plot is woven around an angry goddess who won't let the winds blow the Achaean ships to the sack of Troy unless a king's daughter is slain in human sacrifice! Can such a play be credible to modern readers and theatergoers? How indeed could it have been credible in Euripides' time to Greeks who had outgrown human sacrifice centuries before? One obvious answer is that, as in all Greek tragedies, the dramatist is skilful enough to make the audience accept the conditions of the tragic dilemma as set forth in the myth. But the second reason—related to the first—is that the play really is not about the institution of human sacrifice at all. It might have been, but it isn't. What then is the play about?

One way to approach this question is to start with the characters, especially the two with whom Euripides was obviously deeply involved—the women of the play. There are two of them, in a sense three, though the third never appears. She is Helen of Troy, whom the dramatist never tires of depicting and denouncing both in his dialogue and in his choruses. These characters, all three, sharply contrast with one another. Helen, through selfish love, has brought "travail and trouble" upon all the Greeks. Iphigenia, by selfless sacrifice, rescues the Greek expedition from futility and becomes, so both she and the other characters believe, a "true savior of Greece." Perhaps there is a hint of the meaning of the play in this contrast of the two women. Again the reader or spectator will inevitably compare Iphigenia, the girl who loves her father in spite of his weakness and his intention to kill her, with Clytemnestra, who hates her husband and will one day kill him (as the legend tells us) when he returns from Troy.

Clytemnestra in her speeches of anger and supplication reveals herself in her full tragic stature. Iphigenia's scenes with her father are in a wholly different mood—intimate, affectionate, and pathetic. But they perhaps also point toward what Euripides was saying in the play. She is wholly blind to his weakness. To her—and to her alone in the play—he is a great man, committing her to her death for the sake of Greece. Her attitude toward him is one of love throughout. In an early scene, for example, when father and daughter meet after long absence, she is full of affection and gaiety. But even when she pleads for her life (before she decides to die willingly), her plea is in terms of love and intimacy, not indignation or fear. At the turning point in the play, when she announces her resolve to die, she uses Agamemnon's own words in defense of the war for which she is to die. Finally, in the last scene with her mother, as the play moves toward its tragic end, she asks Clytemnestra not to hate her husband.

Let me clear up one possible misunderstanding. Did Euripides then condone Agamemnon's crime and the injury visited upon his wife Clytemnestra by consenting to the sacrifice of his daughter? Certainly not. No student of this or of his other plays could believe that he did. But perhaps he believed that Iphigenia and Clytemnestra were both "right."

These are, of course, only guesses as to what interested Euripides in this version of the Iphigenia story. Perhaps, somewhere in the death and sacrifice of youth that has occurred in all wars from Troy to Korea lies the meaning—and the mystery—of the play. But how can that be? The sacrifice here is to a divinity "delighting in human blood," and the expedition is led by a wavering and ambitious ruler. Certainly the war will be fought from very mixed motives, some patriotic, some ignoble. All of this was without a doubt also a part of what Euripides was saying, but not all of it, I believe. There is also a blaze of devotion in the play and the mystery of young and *voluntary* dying that has occurred in all periods of human history. Euripides has brought the same theme into other plays but never as the center of dramatic action. As in Shaw's *Saint Joan*, it is as much what Iphigenia's sacrifice does to others as what it does to herself that makes the dramatic moments in the play. This is strikingly true in the scene with Achilles, as well as in the final tragic parting between mother and daughter.

As it has come down to us, the end of the play presents us with a riddle and a challenge. The legendary material contains a variant, probably a later one in mythic history, by which Iphigenia is rescued at the last moment. Miraculously, she is snatched away to live—for a time, at least—in fellowship with the gods, and a hind is slain on the altar instead. In other words, she is not really sacrificed. This "happy ending" has been added by a later interpolator to the text of Euripides' play and appears in all editions. I have followed the practice of most modern translators (Schiller among them) in omitting this happy ending. The whole force of the play collapses if the heroine is hastily caught up to heaven at the last minute. And incidentally, the scene of rescue as reported by the messenger is not only undramatic and unconvincing but spurious. Scholars are unanimous that it is by a later interpolator.

The reader may recall another story of divine rescue of a human victim, the moving story of Abraham and Isaac. But why should that story appear serious and convincing to most people, regardless of their religious faith, but the snatching of Iphigenia as fantasy or fake, as it has to most readers of the play? The reason, I believe, is a fairly obvious one. The Abraham story concerns the problem of faith—faith in Jehovah and utter surrender to his will. But this is only superficially true of Euripides' play. Euripides never for a moment suggests that the goddess should be obeyed out of love or piety. All the arguments for the sacrifice are purely practical, when they are not cynical and self-seeking. It is quite clear that to the playwright it was a crime for Agamemnon to accede to the goddess'—or her priest's—demands. (It is not even clear whether he believes that Artemis has demanded the sacrifice or whether he regards the whole thing as the invention of Calchas, the priest.) The nobility and worth of Iphigenia's action, therefore, is quite independent of either the worthiness of the cause or the motives of those who send her to her death. Her sacrifice is a kind of absolute good that transcends all the rational cynicism around her.

Unhappily this does not rid us of the whole difficulty. There is good evidence that, although the "messenger ending" is spurious, there was once another authentic ending, or "exodus" as the Greeks called the last scene, in which Euripides brought in Artemis herself to resolve the issues of the play and perhaps to explain why a hind was to be substituted for a girl. But what did Euripides actually tell his audience through the mouth of the goddess? We shall probably never know. I am certain, however, that, whatever Euripides wrote, his exodus did not "explain away," as does the interpolated ending, the poetry, the power, or the mystery of the play.

CHARACTERS

Agamemnon, commander-in-chief of the Greek army

Old Man, servant of Agamemnon

Chorus of women of Chalcis who have come to Aulis to see the Greek fleet

Menelaus, brother of Agamemnon, husband of Helen

Clytemnestra, wife of Agamemnon

Iphigenia, daughter of Agamemnon

Orestes (silent)

Messenger

Achilles, future hero of the Trojan war

Attendants, armor-bearers

IPHIGENIA IN AULIS

SCENE: *In front of the tent of Agamemnon, commander of the Greek armies;
on the shore of Aulis' gulf where all the Greek ships lie becalmed.
Agamemnon walks in front of his tent.*

TIME: *Night, just before dawn.*

Agamemnon

Old man, come out in front of the tent.

Old Man (entering)

I'm coming—
What new plan have you got in your head,
My lord Agamemnon?

Agamemnon

Hurry up!

Old Man

I'm hurrying—and I'm not asleep.
Sleep rests light on these old eyes.
I can look sharp.   5

Agamemnon

(*Continues to pace up and down for several
seconds as the Old Man watches him.*)

Well, what is that star
That moves across the sky?

Old Man

That's Sirius, next to the seven Pleiades.
It's still the hour when it rides
Right in the middle of heaven.

Agamemnon

(*Taking his eyes from the sky and listening.*)

No voice is there of birds even,
Or of the seas' waves.

The silence of the winds   10
Holds hushed the river.

Old Man

Yes, but why have you been rushing
Up and down, my lord Agamemnon,
Outside your tent? There's peace
And quiet still over at Aulis
And the guards are quiet too—
Over on the walls of the fort.
They don't move at all. Can we   15
Not go inside now?

Agamemnon

                    I envy you, old man,
I am jealous of men who without peril
Pass through their lives, obscure,
Unknown; least of all do I envy
Those vested with honors.

Old Man

Oh, but these have a glory in their lives!   20

Agamemnon

Ah—a glory that is perilous, and
Will trip them as they walk.
High honors are sweet
To a man's heart, but ever
They stand close to the brink of grief.
Many things can bring calamity.
At one time, it is an enterprise
Of the gods which, failing,
Overturns a man's life. At another,   25
The wills of men, many and malignant,
Ruin life utterly.

Old Man

                    I don't like words
Like these from a king. Agamemnon,

Atreus begat you, but not to have
All good things in your life. No,
It is necessary and it is fated   30
That you be glad and that you
Be sad too, for you were born
Human, and whether you like it or not,
What the gods will comes true.

(*Pause.*)

But you've lit your lamp and
Been writing a letter, haven't you?
You still have it in your hand—   35
With those same words you've
Been putting together. You seal
The letter up—and then tear
The seal open. You've been doing it
Over and over again. Then you
Throw the torch on the ground,
And bulging tears come down out
Of your eyes. My lord, you act   40
Helpless, and mad! What is the pain,
What is the new thing of agony,
O my king! Tell it to me, for I
Am a good man and a loyal servant;
So you can speak. Remember? It was I   45
Who was in the bridal train—
Long ago in the beginning. I was given
To your wife, part of the wedding dowry,
And Tyndareus picked me for this service
Because I was honest.

Agamemnon

(*Explaining the whole situation to the Old Man.*)

Three girls were born to Leda, daughter of Thestius: Phoebe,
Clytemnestra, who is my wife, and Helen. The young men, fore-   50
most in fortune, from all Greece came as Helen's suitors. And each
of them uttered terrible threats against the others, each swearing
he would murder his fellow suitors if he himself failed to

win the girl. Here was her father's dilemma, whether he could   55
best escape disaster at fate's hands by *giving* her or by *not giving* her
in marriage. Then this idea came to him, to bind the suitors by
oath to make a treaty one with another—and seal it with a burnt   60
offering—that whoever won as wife Helen, the child of Tyndareus, that man all the others would defend. If any man should
drive her husband away and steal her from her house, all must
make war upon him and sack his town, whether the town were   65
Greek or barbarian. When they had sworn this, the old man—
tricking them with his strategy—gave his daughter permission to
choose that suitor to whom the sweet breath of love turned her
her heart. So she chose Menelaus—would to God she had not   70
chosen him. Then from Phrygia to Sparta came Paris, who was the
judge of the goddesses—so the Argives have the story. He came
with his garments flowered in gold and his dress blazoned with
barbaric gems. He loved Helen and was loved by her. Then, when   75
her husband was out of the country, he stole her and carried her
off to the herd lands of Ida. Menelaus, stung into fury, ranged
through Greece and invoked that old oath sworn to Tyndareus,
the oath claiming help to avenge this wrong. So all the Greeks   80
sprang to arms, and now they have come to the narrows of Aulis
with all their armament, their ships, their shields, chariots and
horses. And since I am Menelaus' brother, for his sake they chose   85
me as commander-in-chief. Would to God another man had won
that honor.

After the army was mustered in here at Aulis, we were delayed
by the dead calm. It was then the prophet Calchas spoke to all of
us in despair at the weather and urged that my daughter, Iphige-   90
nia, be sacrificed to the goddess of this place. He predicted that
if she were sacrificed we would sail and take and overthrow utterly the land of Troy. But if she were not sacrificed none of these
things would happen. So when I heard this, I ordered our herald,
Talthybius, to make a loud proclamation and dismiss the whole   95
army. I would never have the cruel brutality to kill my own
daughter! After that my brother bore down upon me with arguments of every kind, urging me to commit this horror. Then I

wrote a letter, folded and sealed it, dispatched it to my wife asking
her to send our daughter to be married to Achilles. And in the   100
letter I praised his reputation as a hero and said he would not sail
unless a bride came from our family here to Phthia. I contrived
this deception about the maid's marriage to persuade my wife. Of   105
the Achaeans who know, there are Calchas, Odysseus, and Mene-
laus, only.

   I did this wrong! Now in this letter I rewrite the message and
put down the truth. This I was doing when you saw me in the
dark unsealing the letter and sealing it again. But take the dispatch   110
at once. You must go to Argos! Of the message folded here I will
tell you all, since you are loyal both to my wife and to my house.

Old Man

   Tell me then and show me—so that   115
   The words I speak with my tongue
   Will say these words in the letter.

Agamemnon

                                          (*Nods and reads.*)

   Child of Leda, Clytemnestra:
   This letter will bring you
   A new message, and different
   From the other. Do not send your daughter
   To the calm beach of Aulis, here
   On the Euboean harbor. For we must   120
   Wait another season before we can
   Celebrate our child's marriage.

Old Man

   But when Achilles loses his bride—
   Won't his heart blow up in fierce   125
   Anger against you and against
   Your wife? Oh, this is
   A threatening thing! Tell me
   What you mean by it.

Agamemnon

I'll tell you—
Not in fact but in name only
Is there a marriage with Achilles.
He knows nothing of it or of our plan
Or that I have said I would give him   130
My daughter as his bride.

Old Man

To bring her here a victim then—
A death offering—you promised   135
Her to the son of the goddess!
Oh, you have dared a deed of horror,
My lord Agamemnon!

Agamemnon

My mind is crazed, I fall in ruin!
No—you must get on your way and run.
Forget that your legs are old.

Old Man

I will hurry, my lord.   140

Agamemnon

(*Putting his hands on the Old Man's shoulders.*)

Don't rest by those forest springs
Or give in to sleep.

Old Man

No, no!

Agamemnon

When you come to the fork in the road
Look keenly both ways and be sure   145
The carriage doesn't pass quickly—
When you are not looking—and so
Bring my daughter right to

The Greek ships. And if you
Meet her and her escort,
Turn them back! Yes, take the reins   150
And shake them, send them back
To Argos, back to the city of Cyclops.

Old Man

  I will, my lord!

Agamemnon

  Now, go out from the gates.

Old Man

  Wait. When I say these things,
  Tell me, what will make your wife
  And your daughter trust me?   155

Agamemnon

  This seal. Keep it. It is
  The same as the seal on the letter.
  Now go! The dawn is here, and
  The sun's chariot already is
  Making the day bright. Go—
  And help me out of my trouble.   160

                    (*Old Man goes out.*)

  No mortal man has happiness
  And fortune to the end. He is
  Born, every man, to his grief!

                (*Agamemnon goes out.*)
                   (*Enter Chorus.*)

Chorus

  I have come to the shore
  And the sea sands of Aulis   165
  Over Euripus' waters
  And the sea narrows sailing—
  From Chalcis, my city,

Chalcis, nurse to the fountain
Arethusa, sea surrounded   170
And shining—to see this host
Of noble Achaeans, with their oar-borne ships
Of heroes, whom Menelaus, the yellow-haired   175
And Agamemnon, nobly born—our husbands tell—
Had sent in a thousand galleys
To seek out Helen and seize her;
Helen, whom Paris the herdsman   180
Took from the banks of the river,
Reedy Eurotas, where Aphrodite bestowed her—
On the day when the Cyprian held—
After her dewy bath—
A battle of beauty
With Hera and Pallas Athene.
Through the grove of the victims   185
Artemis' grove I came swift running;
At my eagerness, my cheeks
Reddened with shame—at my yearning to see
The Danaans' fence of shields,
The war gear by each tent,   190
And the great host of armored horsemen.
And now those two whose names are Ajax
I looked upon,
The son of Oileus and Telamon's child
Who is the crown and pride
Of Salamis. Squatting they played at draughts,
Delighting in its trickery.
With them was Protesilaus,   195
With them Palamedes the sea god's son.
Another hurled the discus, Diomedes,   200
And took great joy in it.
Nearby Meriones, Ares' kin,
At whom all mortals marvel.
And from his mountainous island came
Laertes' son and Nireus, goodliest seeming
Of all the Achaeans.   205

Swift-footed Achilles I saw—
His feet like the stormwind—running,
Achilles whom Thetis bore, and
Chiron trained into manhood.
I saw him on the seashore,   210
In full armor over the sands racing.
He strove, his legs in contest
With a chariot and four,
Toward victory racing and rounding
The course. And Eumelus, the Pheretid
Charioteer cried forth in frenzy.   215
I saw his handsome horses there,
Gold-wrought in bits and harness.
Eumelus with his goad struck them,   220
The yoke horses dappled gray,
Their manes white-flecked, and the
Trace horses which flanked them.
Clearly I saw these as they grazed
The post at the end of the race course—   225
They were bays, with their fetlocks
Spotted. And always beside them Peleus' son
Hurled himself onward,
Right by the chariot's car rail,
Right by the spinning axle.   230
And then I came upon the fleet,
An indescribable wonder, so that
With joy my woman's eyes were filled.
The armament of Myrmidons from Phthia
Were there on the right, swift ships, fifty of them.   235
Upon their sterns set high in gold,
The divine daughters of the sea lord   240
Carved as symbols of Achilles' host.
Keel by keel beside them
Lay the Argive ships
Commanded by Mecistes' son,
Whose father Talaus fostered him to manhood.   245
And there was Sthenelus, Capaneus' son.

And leader of the Attic ships in number sixty,
The son of Theseus, who had anchored them
In an even line, and with insignia,
Pallas Athene in her winged car   250
Drawn by the horses of uncloven hoof,
A blessed sign to mariners.

In Boeotia's naval squadron
I counted fifty ships
Fitted with blazonry;   255
Cadmus on each of them
With his golden dragon
High on their poops lifted.
It was Leitus the earth-born
Who commanded the squadron.   260
Next from the land of Phocis
Captain of Locrian ships,
Equal in number was the son of Oileus,
Who had embarked from Thronium,   265
Illustrious city.

From Mycenae, walled by the Cyclops,
The son of Atreus sent his ships,
A hundred galleys in order;
With him his brother,
Commander and friend,
Sailing to wreak revenge on her
Who had fled his hearth   270
To accomplish a foreign marriage.
From Pylus, Gerenian Nestor's
Ships I beheld;
On their poops emblazoned
Bull-bodied Alpheus,   275
Alpheus, the river that runs by his home.
Twelve Aenian ships were there
With Gouneus the king as captain.

Hard by the lords of Elis   280
Whom all men call Epeians;
Their ships Eurytus led,
And led too the Taphian squadron—
Oars gleamed white in the sunlight—
Whose king is Meges, Phyleus' son.   285
They had set sail from the Echinad isles
A rocky terror to mariners.

Ajax, Salamis born,
Linked the right wing of the navy to the left,   290
Knitting together nearest and farthest
Of galleys. And for that linkage
Moved his own twelve ships, easy to pilot.
So the line was unbroken—
Of ships and of shore and of people.   295
No home-going will there be
For any barbarian craft
Which grapples with him there.

The navy's setting forth   300
I've seen it on this day,
So when at home I hear men speak of it,
My vision of the marshaled ships
Will live in memory.

(*Menelaus and the Old Man enter quarreling.*)

Old Man

Menelaus! You have dared a fearful thing
That goes against all conscience.

Menelaus

                              Stand back!
You're a slave—*too* loyal to your master!

Old Man

The insult you've given is honorable.   305

Menelaus

Keep your place—or you'll pay for it in pain.

Old Man

(*Shouting.*)

You had no right to open the letter I carried!

Menelaus

Nor had you the right to carry a message
That brings evil and disaster to all Greece.

Old Man

I'll argue that with others—give me the letter.

Menelaus

I will not give it.   310

Old Man

                And I won't let it go!

Menelaus

This stick will beat your head into a bloody pulp.

Old Man

To die for my lord would be a good death.

Menelaus

Hands off—you talk too much for a slave.

(*Enter Agamemnon.*)

Old Man

O my king, look how I am wronged!
He took me by force—and tore your letter   315
From my hand. Now, he won't listen to right
Or to reason.

Agamemnon

                What is this—a brawl
And argument right at my own door?

Menelaus

> Before this man is heard I have the right
> To speak.

Agamemnon

> What brought you into the scuffle—
> And why abuse him with such violence?

> *(The Old Man goes out.)*

Menelaus

> First, look upon my face, Agamemnon,   320
> Then I will begin to tell my story.

Agamemnon

> I am the son of Atreus. Do you think
> He shrinks from *your* eye, Menelaus?

Menelaus

> *(Impatiently.)*

> This letter carries a message of treason!

Agamemnon

> I see the letter—First, give it to me—

Menelaus

> Not till I've shown its message to all Greeks.

Agamemnon

> So now you know what you have no right   325
> To know. You broke the seal!

Menelaus

> Yes, I broke it
> And to your sorrow. You'll suffer now
> For the evil you secretly plotted!

Agamemnon

> Where did you find him? Oh, you have no shame!

Menelaus

I was watching to see if your daughter
Had arrived at the camp out of Argos.

Agamemnon

It's true—you have no shame. What reason
Have you for spying in my affairs?

Menelaus

My own desire
Urged me. I am not a slave of yours.   330

Agamemnon

Can there be any outrage like this?
You won't allow me to rule in my own house!

Menelaus

No, for your mind is treacherous. One day
You plan one thing, another day another,
Tomorrow you will shift again.

Agamemnon

You frame
The lies neatly. Oh, I hate a smooth tongue!

Menelaus

Agamemnon,
A disloyal heart is false to friends and
A thing of evil. Now *you* I want to question,   335
And don't, because you are angry, turn your face
From the truth—I shall not rack you too hard.
Have you forgotten when you were eager
And anxious to lead the Greek army to Troy,
Wanting to appear unambitious but in your heart
Eager for command? Do you remember how humble
You were to all the people, grasping the hand,
Keeping open the doors of your house, yes,   340

Open to all, granting to every man, even the lowly,
The right to address and to hail you by name?
These ways and tricks you tried, to buy
In the market advancement, but when at last
You won power, then you turned these habits
Of your heart inside out. Now were you
No longer loving to your friends of yesterday.
No—the old ones could not reach you, but,
Unapproachable, you were seldom found at home.   345
Oh, it is vile for a man, if he be noble,
And when he has won to the heights of power,
To put on new manners for old and change
His countenance. Far more when he's in fortune
And able truly to succor, must he hold
Firmly to old friends. This is the good man's
Character. So I blame you for these things
Where first I found you ignoble. And then
You came to Aulis with the army—   350
The Panhellenic host! And suddenly—
From being all, you became nothing,
Confounded by a fate God-given, lacking
But this one thing: a favoring wind
To dispatch the fleet. So the Danaans urged
That you send back every ship and at Aulis
Put an end to this toil without meaning.
I remember your face then, bewildered,
Unhappy, fearing you would never captain
Your thousand ships or fill up with spears   355
The fields of Priam's Troy. Then you called me
Into council. What shall I do? you asked me.
What scheme, what strategy can I devise
That will prevent the stripping-off
Of my command and the loss of my glorious name?

Calchas spoke: Sacrifice on the altar
Your own daughter to Artemis, and the Greek ships

Will sail. At that instant your heart filled up
With gladness and happily, in sacrifice,   360
You promised to slay the child. So you
Sent willingly to your wife, not by compulsion—
You cannot deny that—that she send the girl
Here, and for pretext, that she come to marry
Achilles. This is the very air which heard
These words from your mouth. But then, turning
Your mind about, in secret you recast
The message. So now your story?—you will
Never be your daughter's murderer! I tell you   365
Thousands have done what you have done. Willingly
Worked and striven up to the peaks of power,
Then in the flush of attainment, they fail
And fall in ignominy. Now in some instances
The populace is responsible out of stupidity,
But with other men the failure is in them,
Impotent—like you—to lead or protect
The state. Oh, chiefly in this present case
I groan for Greece in her affliction,   370
For she was ready to act with honor,
But on account of your girl and you,
She lets the barbarians, even the basest
Of them, slip from her grasp and make her name
A mockery! O may I never make
Any man ruler of my country or
Commander of her armies because I am
In debt to him. No, a general
Must have wit; and a ruler, understanding.   375

Chorus

Terrible are these fighting words which lead
Brothers into strife with one another.

Agamemnon

Now will I give you briefly *my* reproach.
Nor will my looks grow haughty with contempt,

But looking and speaking I'll be temperate,
As it befits a brother and as a good man   380
To another shows decency and respect.
Your eyes are bloodshot—and what
Dire threats are these? Tell me, who
Has wronged you, what do you want? Are you
Burning to possess a virtuous wife? Well,
I can't procure her for you. The one you had
You governed foully. Should I pay the price
For these your sins, when I am innocent?
Or is it my advancement that bites your heart?   385
No, you've thrown to the winds all reason
And honor, and lust only to hold a lovely woman
In your arms. Oh, the pleasures of the base
Are always vile. And now—if yesterday
I was without wit or wisdom, but today
Have counseled with myself well and wisely—
Does that make me mad? Rather are you crazed,
For the gods, being favorable, rid you of
A wicked wife, and now you want her back!   390
As to the suitors, marriage-mad, with evil
In their hearts, they swore an oath to Tyndareus.
Yes, I grant that, but a crazed hope which
I believe a god inspired effected all,
Not any influence or strength in you.
Make war with them—they'll join you in their folly!   395
But in heaven there is intelligence—it can
Perceive oaths bonded in evil, under compulsion
Sworn. *So I will not kill my children.*
Nor will your enterprise of vengeance upon
An evil wife prosper against all justice.
If I did commit this act, against law, right,
And the child I fathered, each day, each night,
While I yet lived would wear me out in grief
And tears. So these are my few words, clear   400
And easily understood. You may choose madness,
But I will order my affairs in decency and honor.

Chorus

   How different are these words from those you spoke
Before—but it is good to save the child.

Menelaus

   O gods—so now I have *no* friends.

Agamemnon

   And you'll have none while you try to destroy them.   405

Menelaus

   Where is the proof you are our father's son,
My brother?

Agamemnon

             I am brother to you
When you are sane, not mad.

Menelaus

                    Should not
A friend share with friends his grief?

Agamemnon

   Speak when you have befriended me,
Not done me injury.

Menelaus

                Greece is in grief   410
And in trouble. Isn't it right that you
Should bear a part of the hardship?

Agamemnon

   This is what I think—Greece, like yourself,
Some god has driven mad.

Menelaus

               You have a king's
Scepter—boast of it and puff yourself up!

To me you are a traitor, so I'll turn
To other means and other friends.

(*Enter Messenger.*)

Messenger

O commander of all the armies of Greece,
King Agamemnon, I am here to bring   415
To you your daughter, Iphigenia,
And her mother who is with her,
The queen, Clytemnestra.
And the boy Orestes is here—you've been
So long from home that, seeing him, delight
Will fill your heart.

Now after weary travel, beside a stream   420
Free flowing, the ladies rest and bathe
Their feet. So do the horses! On the green
Meadow we've turned them loose to browse.

I have come, running ahead of the others
To prepare you with this information:
Rumor travels fast and by now the army   425
Knows that your daughter has arrived in Aulis.
In fact, crowds from the camp already have come
On the run for a sight of the maiden.
For the highborn are glorious and all men
Gaze at them. Now they are saying: Is it
A marriage, or what happens now?   430
Has King Agamemnon so yearned in love
For his daughter that now he has brought her
To Aulis? This too you could hear them say:
Men make the marriage offering to Artemis,
Aulis' queen, but who will be the bridegroom?

(*He smiles.*)

Shall we prepare barley for sacrifice?   435
Let us crown our heads with garlands, and you,
King Menelaus, start the bridal hymn!

Oh, let the lutes be played, and there should be
Dancing within the pavilion, since for
The maid this day should dawn in happiness.

Agamemnon

(Stiffly.)

You are thanked for your news. Now you may go   440
Within the pavilion. As to the rest—
It will go well as the fates will it.

(The Messenger goes out.)

O God, how can I find words or begin
To speak in the face of this, my disaster?
Fallen into the pit, fate chains me there.
I forged a conspiracy, but shrewder far
A hundred times were the stratagems   445
Which Fate invented. O fortunate men of mean,
Ignoble birth, freely you may weep and
Empty out your hearts, but the highborn—
Decorum rules our lives and we, by service
To the mob, become its slaves.   450

                         Look at me, brother.
I am ashamed of these tears. And yet
At the extremity of my misfortune
I am ashamed not to shed them. What words
Can I utter to my wife or with what countenance
Receive and welcome her when she appears,   455
Unsummoned, in the midst of my disaster?
Yet coming she only obeys nature,
Following a daughter here to do love's services,
And give the bride away. So doing, she
Shall find me out the author of this evil.

And the unhappy maiden! Maiden, no—   460
Soon, it seems, Hades will marry her.
Oh, piteous fate! I hear her cries to me;

O Father, why do you kill me? May Death
Be your bride also and betroth
All of your dear ones as he has plighted me!
Beside her, Orestes the infant will cry out   465
Meaningless words, but full of meaning
To my heart!
O Paris, Helen, it is your marrying
Which has wrought these things
And my damnation!

Chorus

And I too grieve, so far as a stranger may,
Over a king's misfortune.   470

Menelaus

My brother, grant me this, to grasp your hand—

Agamemnon

Here it is. You have won the mastery.
I now face the ordeal of my defeat.

Menelaus

No! I swear by Pelops, father of our
Father, and by Atreus, who begat us both,
That truly now I do not speak toward
Any end but inwardly and from my heart.   475
When I saw tears bursting from your eyes
Tears started in mine and a great pity
Seized me. I am no longer terrible   480
To you, or any more your enemy.
All the words spoken I now withdraw, and
From them I retreat. I stand in your place
And beseech you do not slay the child
To prosper me and to destroy yourself.
It is against all justice that you should
Groan from the same cause that makes me

Fortunate or that your daughter die while
All my children live and face the sun.
What do I want? Could I not obtain   485
A perfect marriage elsewhere, if I longed for
Marrying? But a brother whom I should
Most cherish, I was about to forfeit
To gain a Helen, so bartering excellence
For evil. I was witless and adolescent
Until, crowding upon the deed, I saw and knew
All that it meant to kill the child.   490
Besides this, thinking upon our kinship,
Pity for the girl in her harsh agony
Swept over me: she would be killed
On account of my marriage. But what has Helen
To do with this girl of yours? Disband
The host, I say, let it go from Aulis,   495
And so cease drowning your eyes in tears
Or summoning me to grieve and weep for you.
As to your share and mine in the oracle
Concerning your daughter's destiny, I
Want no part in it; my share I give to you.
And so I've turned my threatening words   500
Into their opposites! But it is fitting;
I have changed because I love a brother.
To seek, as here I have done, always
For the best action in the case is *not*
The character of an evil man!

Chorus

O King, you honor your forefathers—   505
A speech worthy of Tantalus, Zeus' son.

Agamemnon

I thank you, Menelaus, that now
Beyond my hopes you have spoken justly,
With right reason, worthy of yourself.

« 238 »

These quarrels between brothers spring from
Many things, over a woman, for instance,
Or out of greed for the inheritance.
I loathe them all. Such kinships pour bitterness   510
Into both hearts. But we have arrived
At a fatal place: A compulsion absolute
Now works the slaughter of the child.

Menelaus

What do you mean? Who will force you to kill her?

Agamemnon

The whole concourse of Achaean armies.

Menelaus

No—not if you send her back to Argos.   515

Agamemnon

I might do it secretly—but from the army
I could not keep the secret.

Menelaus
                                        You are wrong
To fear the mob so desperately.

Agamemnon

Listen to me. To the whole Greek army
Calchas will report the prophecy.

Menelaus

No, not if Calchas, the prophet, is first dead,
And that will be quite simple to accomplish.

Agamemnon

How arrogant they are! The whole race of prophets—   520
A curse upon this earth.

Menelaus

They're of no value
To man, or use whatever, especially when alive.

Agamemnon

Menelaus, do you feel none of the terror
Which creeps into my heart?

Menelaus

How can I know
Your fear if you do not name it?

Agamemnon

Odysseus,
Son of Sisyphus, *knows* all these things.

Menelaus

Odysseus is not such a man or personage   525
That he can harm you or me.

Agamemnon

He is cunning
In his tactics always and his ear
Is close to the mob.

Menelaus

It's his ambition,
An evil and a cursed thing, piercing
His very soul.

Agamemnon

I agree—so will he not
Stand up in the midst of the army and
Tell the prophecy which Calchas spoke
And how I promised to sacrifice   530
My victim to Artemis—and how I then
Annulled my promises? Oh, with these words
Will he arouse and seize the very soul

Of the army, order them to kill you
And me—and sacrifice the girl.

If I should escape to Argos they then
Would follow me there, and even to
The Cyclopean walls to raze them
To the earth and the land destroy utterly.   535
Such is the terrible circumstance in which
I find myself. Now in my despair I am
Quite helpless, and it is God's will.

(*He bows his head for a moment*
in despair, then looks up.)

Do this one thing for me, Menelaus,
Go to the army, take all precaution
That Clytemnestra learn nothing of this
Till after I have seized the child and   540
Sent her to her death. So I may do
This evil—which I have to do—
With fewest tears. And you, ladies, who are
Our guests, see that you guard your lips.

(*Agamemnon and Menelaus go out.*)

Chorus

O blest are those who share
In Aphrodite's gifts   545
With modesty and measure,
Blest who escape the frenzied passion
For Eros of the golden hair
Shoots his two arrows of desire,
And the one brings happiness   550
To man's life, the other ruin.
O Cypris, loveliest of goddesses
In heaven, keep this frenzied arrow
From my heart.
Keep modest my delights

All my desires lawful,   555
So may I have my part in love
But not in passion's madness.

Many are the natures of men,
Various their manners of living,
Yet a straight path is always the right one;   560
And lessons deeply taught
Lead man to paths of righteousness;
Reverence, I say, is wisdom
And by its grace transfigures—
So that we seek virtue
With a right judgment.   565
From all of this springs honor
Bringing ageless glory into
Man's life. Oh, a mighty quest
Is the hunting out of virtue—
Which for womankind
Must be a love in quietness,
But, for men, infinite are the ways   570
To order and augment
The state.
O Paris, you returned to
The land which reared you,
Herdsman of white heifers
Upon Ida's mountains; where   575
Barbarian melodies you played
Upon a Phrygian flute
And echoed there once more
Olympus' pipe.

Full-uddered cattle browsed
When the goddesses summoned you   580
For this trial of beauty—
Trial which sent you
To Greece, to knock at the doors
Of ivory palaces; it was there

Looking into Helen's eyes
You gave and took the ecstasies of love.   585
So from this quarrel came
The assault by Greeks
With ship and spear
Upon Troy's citadel.

(Turning, they see Queen Clytemnestra
and Iphigenia in a chariot,
approaching.)

O august ladies,   590
Daughters of the mighty of the earth,
How blest you are! Behold
Iphigenia, the king's daughter,
And Clytemnestra, queen,
Daughter of Tyndareus.
They, sprung from the mighty ones,
Ride on to highest destiny.   595
The gods themselves, bestowers of happiness,
They are not more august
Than these
The fortunate amongst mankind.

Now let us stand here, children of Chalcis,
Let us receive the queen
Out of her chariot
And keep her step from stumbling   600
To the earth.

(Enter, riding in a chariot, Clytemnestra, Iphigenia,
and the young child, Orestes. Attendants
accompany them.)

Gently, but with good will,
And with our hands
We will help you down.
O noble daughter of Agamemnon,
Newly come to Aulis, have no fear!

For to you, stranger from Argos— 605
Gently and without clamor
We who are strangers too
Give you our welcome.

Clytemnestra

I shall think of this as a good omen—
Your kindness and good words—for I am here,
Hopefully, to lead this young girl 610
Into a noble and a happy marriage.
Now, will you take the dowry from the wagon—
All of her bridal gifts which I have brought.
Carry them into the pavilion carefully.
And you, daughter, put down your pretty feet
And get out of the carriage. All of you
Maidens take her into your arms and help 615
Her down.

(Smiling and matter of fact.)

And now, will someone lend me
The support of an arm, that with greater
Ease I may dismount—stand in front, please,
Of the horses' yoke—see the colt's eyes are 620
Wild with terror!

(After the horse has been steadied.)

Now, this is Agamemnon's son.
Take him—his name is Orestes—and he's
Still quite a helpless baby. My baby,
Are you still asleep from the rolling wheels?
Wake up and be happy. This is your sister's
Wedding day! You are noble, and so
You will have a nobleman as kin, 625
The godlike child of the Nereid.
My child, Iphigenia, come sit next to
Your mother. Stay close beside me and show
All these strangers here how happy and how

Blessed I am in you! But here he comes—
Your most beloved father. Go, give him welcome.   630

> (*Enter Agamemnon.*)

Iphigenia

O Mother, don't be angry if I run
Ahead and throw myself into his arms.

> (*Attendants go out, one of them carrying
> Orestes in her arms.*)

Clytemnestra

Mightiest and most honored, Lord Agamemnon,
Obedient to your command, we are here.

Iphigenia

Father!
I long to throw myself before anyone   635
Into your arms—it's been so long a time—
And kiss your cheek! Oh, are you angry, Mother?

Clytemnestra

No my child, this is rightful, and it is
As it has always been. Of all the children
I have borne your father, you love him most.

Iphigenia

Father, what a desperate age since I   640
Saw you last! But now, seeing you again,
I am happy.

Agamemnon

> And I, seeing you,
Am happy. You speak for both of us, Iphigenia.

Iphigenia

> (*Smiling and laughing.*)

Hail! O Father, it is a good and
Wonderful thing you have done—bringing me here!

Agamemnon

I do not know how to answer what you say,
My child.

Iphigenia

Oh? You say you are glad to see me,
But your eyes have no quiet in them.

Agamemnon

I have cares—the many cares of a general   645
And a king.

Iphigenia

Oh, turn away from all of them,
My father—be here and mine only, now!

Agamemnon

I am. Now I am nowhere but in this place,
And with you utterly, my darling.

Iphigenia

Oh then,
Unknit your brow.

(Putting her hand on his forehead.)
And smooth your face for love.

Agamemnon

Now see my joy as I look at you—

Iphigenia

And yet,
The tears—a libation of tears—are there   650
Ready to pour from your eyes.

Agamemnon

Well,
There is a long parting about to come
For both of us—

Iphigenia
> I don't understand,
> Dear Father—I don't understand—

Agamemnon
> And yet
> You do seem to speak with understanding,
> And I am the more grieved.

Iphigenia
> I'll speak foolishly
> If that will please you more.

Agamemnon
> (*To himself.*)
> How hard to curb my tongue! 655
> (*Aloud.*)
> Yes, do.

Iphigenia
> Now for a time, Father dear, won't you stay
> At home with your children?

Agamemnon
> O that I might!
> This willing and not doing will crack my heart.

Iphigenia
> Menelaus' wrongs and his spearmen—O
> That they'd disappear!

Agamemnon
> He and his wrongs
> Will destroy others first—then ruin me.

Iphigenia
> (*Still preoccupied with her absence from him.*)
> Father, you've been so long in Aulis' gulf! 660

Agamemnon

                               I must

  Equip and dispatch the armies, I am still
  Hindered and held up.

Iphigenia

                      Where is it they say
  These Trojans live, my father?

Agamemnon

                      In the country
  Where Paris, the son of Priam, dwells, and
  Would to heaven he had never lived at all!

Iphigenia

  You're going on a long voyage, *leaving me!*

Agamemnon

                    (Speaking to himself.)

  But your situation is like mine, my daughter—   665
  You're going on a long voyage—leaving your father.

Iphigenia

  Oh—on this voyage of *yours* I only wish
  It were right for you to take me with you!

Agamemnon

  It is ordained that you too take a long
  Sailing, my daughter, to a land where—where
  You must remember me!

Iphigenia

                  Shall I go
  On this voyage with my mother, or alone?

Agamemnon

  Alone—Cut off and quite separated
  From both your father and your mother.

Iphigenia

A new home you make for me, Father,   670
Where will it be?

Agamemnon

Now stop—it's not right
For a girl to know all of these things.

Iphigenia

Father, over there when you have done
All things well, hurry back to me from Troy!

Agamemnon

(*Driven by an inner compulsion to speak
what he knows he must conceal.*)

I will, but first, right here, in Aulis
I must offer sacrifice.

Iphigenia

Oh yes, of course,
With sacrifices we must pay homage to heaven.

Agamemnon

(*Hypnotized by his own thoughts.*)

You shall see this one, for you are to stand   675
By the basin of holy water.

Iphigenia

Then round the altar shall I start the dance?

Agamemnon

O for this happy ignorance that is yours!
Now go into the pavilion and be
Alone with your maidens. Give me a kiss
Of pain and your right hand, for soon you go
To live apart from your father. And this   680
Will be too long a parting!

(*Holding her in his arms.*)

O breast and cheeks! O golden hair!
What bitter burden Helen and her Troy city
Have laid upon you! I must stop, for as I
Touch you my eyes are water springs—the tears
Start their escape. Go into the pavilion!   685

(*Iphigenia goes out.*)

Oh, forgive me, child of Leda, for this
Self-pity! Here am I giving in marriage
My daughter to Achilles! Such partings
Bring happiness but prick the heart of a father
Who, after all his fostering care, must give
Away a daughter to another's home.   690

Clytemnestra

I am not unfeeling, nor do I reproach
Your grief. For I, too, shall sorrow
As I lead her and as the marriage hymn is sung.
But time and custom will soften sadness.
His name to whom you have betrothed   695
Our child I know. Now tell me
His home and lineage.

Agamemnon

Asopus had a daughter, Aegina—

Clytemnestra

Yes, who married her, god or a mortal?

Agamemnon

Zeus married her. Aeacus was their son
And he became Oenone's husband.

Clytemnestra

Tell me,
Which child of Aeacus received the inheritance?   700

Agamemnon

   Peleus—he married Nereus' daughter.

Clytemnestra

   Did the gods bless their marriage
   Or did he take her against their will?

Agamemnon

   Zeus betrothed her and the lord Nereus
   Gave her away in marriage.

Clytemnestra

                Tell me—
   Where did he marry her? Under the sea's waves?

Agamemnon

   No, on the holy foothills of Pelion,   705
   Where Chiron lives.

Clytemnestra

            It is there the tribes
   Of Centaurs make their home?

Agamemnon

              Yes, and it was there
   The gods gave Peleus a marriage feast.

Clytemnestra

   Will you tell me this—did Thetis rear
   Achilles or his father?

Agamemnon

         Chiron taught him,
   That he might never learn the customs of
   Evil men.

Clytemnestra

      I would say a wise teacher, but
   Peleus giving him that teacher was wiser still.   710

Agamemnon

    So, such a man is your daughter's husband.

Clytemnestra

    A perfect choice! Where is his city in Greece?

Agamemnon

    It is within Phthia; and beside
    The river Apidanus—

Clytemnestra

                 And it's there
    That you will bring your child and mine?   715

Agamemnon

    That should be her husband's care.

Clytemnestra

    Well, I ask heaven's blessings upon them—
    What is the day set for the marriage?

Agamemnon

    When the full moon comes, to bring them good luck.

Clytemnestra

    Now I ask this, have you slain the victims
    To Artemis, the goddess, for our child?

Agamemnon

    I shall, I have made all the preparations.

Clytemnestra

    And then you will hold the marriage feast?   720

Agamemnon

    When I've sacrificed to the gods their due.

Clytemnestra

   And where do *I* make the women's feast?

Agamemnon

   Here, by these proud sterns of our ships.

Clytemnestra

   By the anchors and hawsers? Well,
   May good fortune come of it?

Agamemnon

                        My lady,
   This you must do—Obey!   725

Clytemnestra

                     That is no revelation—
   I am accustomed to it.

Agamemnon

                  So here
   Where the bridegroom is I will—

Clytemnestra

                        Do what?
   You'll take what office that is mine?

Agamemnon

                           I shall
   Give the child away—with the Danaan's help.

Clytemnestra

   And meantime, where must *I* be staying?   730

Agamemnon

   In Argos, where you must take care
   Of your younger daughters.

Clytemnestra

                        Leaving the child?
   Who then will lift the marriage torch?

Agamemnon

Whatever torch is fitting, I will raise it.

Clytemnestra

Against all custom! And you see
Nothing wrong in that?

Agamemnon

I see that it is
Wrong for you to stay, mingling with the host   735
Of the army—

Clytemnestra

I think it *right*
A mother give away her daughter.

Agamemnon

But wrong, I tell you, to leave the maidens
Alone in our halls.

Clytemnestra

In maiden chambers
They are safe and well guarded.

Agamemnon

Obey me!

Clytemnestra

No! by the Argive's goddess queen!
You go outside and do your part, I indoors   740
Will do what's proper for the maid's marrying.

(*Clytemnestra goes out.*)

Agamemnon

Oh, I have rushed madly into this and failed
In every hope: desiring to send my wife
Out of my sight—I a conspirator
Against my best beloved and weaving plots

Against her. Now I am confounded 745
In all things. Yet to the priest Calchas
I will go, with him to ask the goddess' pleasure
Though that should spell my doom,
And for Greece toil and travail.
A wise man keeps his wife at home
Virtuous and helpful—or never marries. 750

(Agamemnon goes out.)

Chorus

Now will they come to Simois
And the silvery swirl of her waters—
The Greeks mighty in assembly
With their ships and their armor;
To Ilium, to the plains of Troy 755
Sacred to Phoebus Apollo,
Where Cassandra is prophet, I hear,
Her head green crowned with the laurel—
And wildly she flings her golden hair
As the god breathes in her soul 760
The frenzy of foresight.

Upon the battle towers of Troy,
Around her walls, Trojans will stand
When Ares in harness of bronze
On these stately ships over the sea 765
Moves to the runnels of Simois.
Oh, he'll come desiring the seizure of Helen
To hale her from Priam's palace, 770
She whose brothers are Zeus' sons—
Dioscuri are their name stars in heaven—
To hale Helen to the land of Greece
By toil of battle
And the shields and spears of Achaeans.

Pergamus with walls of stone, Phrygia's town,
He will encircle in bloody battle, 775

Cutting the defenders' throats,
To drag their bodies headless away;
Then from the citadel's top peak to earth
He will sack all the dwellings in Troy city.
So every maiden will wail loudly,
And with them Priam's queen.   780
And Helen too, who is daughter of Zeus,
She will cry aloud,
Who in the years gone had forsaken her husband.
Oh, we who are women of Chalcis
May this fate never be ours   785
Or that of our children's children!
To be as the golden Lydian ladies,
Or the Phrygian wives—
To stand before their looms
And wail to one another:

"Who will lay hands on my shining hair,   790
When tears flood my eyes,
And who will pluck me a flower
Out of my country's ruin?
Oh it is on account of *you*,
Child of the arch-necked swan,
If the story is to be believed,
The story that Leda bore you to a winged bird,   795
To Zeus himself transformed!
But perhaps this is a fable
From the book of the Muses
Borne to me out of season,   800
A senseless tale."

                              (*Achilles enters.*)

Achilles

Where is the commander-in-chief?
Will one of his aides give him this message
That Achilles, the son of Peleus is here
At the door of his pavilion.

*(After a pause, turns and speaks what
is on his mind to the Chorus.)*

This delay by the river Euripus
Is not alike for all, let me tell you.
Some of us are unmarried. We've simply   805
Abandoned our halls and sit here idly
On the beaches. Others have left at home
Their wives and children, all because
A terrible passion has seized all Greece
To make this expedition—not without
Heaven's contrivance. Whatever others
May argue, I'll tell *my* righteous grievance!   810
I left Pharsalia and my father Peleus,
And here by the Euripus I must wait—
Wait because here these light winds blow—
And curb my own troops, my Myrmidons.
They are forever urging me and saying:
We are the army for Troy! How many months   815
Must we drag out here? Act if you are going
To act, if not, wait no longer upon
Atreus' sons and on their dallyings
But lead the army home.

> *(Clytemnestra enters from the pavilion.)*

Clytemnestra

Son of the Nereid, I come to greet you—
I heard your voice inside the tent.   820

Achilles

O august lady—Whom do my eyes meet,
A woman peerless in her loveliness!

Clytemnestra

It is not marvelous that you do not know me
Since into my presence you never came before.

> *(Smiling.)*

But I praise your respect for modesty.

Achilles

    Who are you? And why, lady, have you come   825
    To the mustering-in of the Greek army—
    You, a woman, into a camp of armed men?

Clytemnestra

    I am the daughter of Leda, Clytemnestra.
    Agamemnon is my husband.

Achilles

                      My lady,
    You have spoken what was fitting
    With brevity and beauty, but for me
    I may not rightly hold converse here   830
    With you or any woman—

                          (He starts to leave.)

Clytemnestra

    Oh wait! Why rush away? With your
    Right hand clasp mine and let this be
    The beginning of a blest betrothal.

Achilles

    What are you saying, Queen Clytemnestra?
    I take your right hand in mine? That is
    Wrongful—I would be ashamed before the king.

Clytemnestra

    It is wholly right, child of the Nereid,   835
    Since soon you will marry my daughter.

Achilles

                    What!
    What marriage do you speak of, my lady?

                    (After a moment's pause.)

    I have no word to put into my answer,
    Unless this I say—from some strange frenzy
    Of your mind you have conceived this story—

Clytemnestra

    By nature all men are shy, seeing new
    Kinsmen, or hearing talk of marriage.   840

Achilles

    My lady, never have I courted your daughter,
    Or from the sons of Atreus either
    Has ever word of this marriage come to me.

Clytemnestra

                           (Deeply troubled.)

    I do not understand—I am amazed at your words—

Achilles

    Let's search this out together for there may   845
    Be truth in what we both have said.

Clytemnestra

    Oh, I have been horribly abused!
    The betrothal which I came here to find,
    At Aulis, never existed here or anywhere
    But is a lie—Oh, I am crushed with shame!

Achilles

    My lady, perhaps it is only this:
    Someone is laughing at us both.
    But I beg of you: take any mockery
    Without concern, and bear it lightly.   850

Clytemnestra

    Farewell! Deceived as I am, humiliated,
    I can no longer lift my eyes to yours.

Achilles

    I too bid you farewell, my lady,
    And go now into the tent to seek your husband.

Old Man

(Calling from within the tent.)

Sir, wait! I'm calling to you there—O   855
Grandson of Aeacus, child of the goddess,
And you, my lady, daughter of Leda!

Achilles

Who shouts through the open door—and in terror?

Old Man

I am a slave. I cannot boast to you
Of my position—that is my fate.

Achilles

Whose slave? Not mine, he would not be here
In Agamemnon's retinue.

Old Man

I belong

To the lady who stands before this tent   860
A gift to her from her father, Tyndareus.

Achilles

I wait. Now say why you hold me here.

Old Man

Are both of you alone before the doors?

Achilles

We are. Speak and come out from the royal tent.

Old Man (*entering*)

May Fate and my good foresight rescue you!

Achilles

(To Clytemnestra.)

The man's story—it tells something   865
About to happen and I think important—

Clytemnestra

Speak, old man, don't wait to kiss my hand.

Old Man

You know who I am, my lady, loyal
To you and to your children?

Clytemnestra

Yes, I know,
You were an old house servant in the palace.

Old Man

King Agamemnon took me as a portion
In your dowry.

Clytemnestra

Yes, yes, and coming to Argos   870
With us, you have been mine ever since.

Old Man

That is the truth, and I am more loyal
To you than to your husband—

Clytemnestra

Now the mystery
You have been guarding, out with it!

Old Man

(*Trembling as he speaks.*)

I'll tell you quickly. Her father plans
With his own hand to kill your child.

Clytemnestra

What words of a crazed mind
Have come out of your mouth, old man.

Old Man

It is true—with a knife at her white throat   875
He will kill her.

Clytemnestra
>Oh, how miserable am I!
He has been stricken, then, with madness?

Old Man
No. In all other things, my queen,
Your lord is sane except in this obsession
Toward you and toward the child.

Clytemnestra
Why? *Why?* What is the demon of vengeance
Which drives him to this horror?

Old Man
The oracle is the demon, the oracle
Which Calchas spoke telling how the fleet may sail—

Clytemnestra
Her father will kill her! O gods, what a fate   880
And affliction for me and for the child.
You say the fleet? Where will it sail?

Old Man
To the lords of Troy and to their halls
So that Menelaus may bring Helen back.

Clytemnestra
Oh, fate then has bound Helen's homecoming
To my daughter and to her death.

Old Man
You know all of the mystery now, and that
It is to Artemis that her father
Will sacrifice the child.

Clytemnestra

(*Her voice hard and full of hate.*)

And the marriage,
That was the pretext which he invented
To bring me from Argos.

Old Man

Yes, and the king
Calculated that you would bring her gladly   885
To be the bride of Achilles.

Clytemnestra

O Daughter,
We have been escorted, you and with you
Your mother, to death and to destruction.

Old Man

The fate of the child is pitiable
And yours too, my queen. The king
Has dared a deed of horror.

Clytemnestra

Now, I cannot
Hold them back, these streams of tears. I am lost,
Utterly.

Old Man

What greater cause, my lady,
For grieving than a child taken away?
Weep, weep.

Clytemnestra

(*Suddenly controlling herself.*)

These plans—how do you know them   890
For the truth? Where did you find out these things,
Old man?

Old Man

I'll tell you. I was on my way, running
To bring you the letter, a second to
Follow the first from my lord Agamemnon—

Clytemnestra

And my husband's word to bring the girl—
To bring her to her death—did he confirm
The message?

Old Man

No. He said *not* to bring her,
For this second time he wrote sanely and
In his right mind.

Clytemnestra

Oh, why didn't you deliver *that* letter?

Old Man

Because Menelaus tore it out of my hand,   895
And he is the cause of all our ruin.

Clytemnestra

(*Turning to Achilles.*)

Child of the Nereid, Peleus' son, do you hear?

Achilles

I hear the story of your fate and misery
And I cannot bear my part in it.

Clytemnestra

They use this trick of your marriage
To slaughter my child!

Achilles

Now lady, let me
Hurl *my* reproach upon your husband—

Clytemnestra

(Falling on her knees to him.)

Oh, you were born of a goddess, I—
I am mortal but I am not ashamed   900
To clasp your knees or to do eagerly
This or anything that will bring succor
For my daughter's sake. Protect us both—
Me from my evil fate, and she, defend her
Who is your betrothed, even though the
Marriage may never be. In name only
Is she your bride, and yet, I led her here
To be your wife and crowned her head   905
With a bride's wreath.

                Oh, I have brought her
Not for marrying but for death and sacrifice!
Son of the goddess, a shameful reproach
Will be yours if you do not shield her!
Although no marriage yokes you
To the unhappy girl, yet to all men,
You are her lord and her dear husband.
Listen to me—since through your name   910
You have brought my undoing and my end,
I beg you, by your beard, your right hand, and
By your mother's name—O cleanse your own
Name of this reproach!

Child of the goddess, I have no altar
To which I can flee for safety except
To your knees, and I have no friends to help me
In this distant place. You have heard
The strategy, which is savage and shameless,
Of Agamemnon the king, and you see
How I have come, a woman and helpless,
Into a camp of men, sailors of the fleet,
Eager for any violence and yet

Strong to save and help if it come
Into their hearts. Oh—if you have the courage,   915
Now stretch out your hand and surely I am
Saved, but if you do not dare it—I am lost!

Chorus

Oh, what a power is motherhood, possessing
A potent spell. All women alike
Fight fiercely for a child.

Achilles

At your words in pride and in anger
My soul is lifted up.[1]
Our generals, the Atreidae, I obey
When their command is righteous, but
When evil, I shall not obey, and here
As in Troy, I shall show my nature free   930
To fight my enemy with honor.

But you, lady, suffer things savage and cruel
Even from those you love, so with my compassion
Which I put around you like a shield
I shall make right these wrongs abominable
As far as a young man can.
I tell you—never will your daughter   935
Who is my betrothed—die murdered by
Her father's hand. Nor to this conspiracy
Of your husband will I offer my name or
My person. He has planned it guiltily
In this fashion that though my sword
Is not drawn, my name, my name only
Will kill the child. Oh, then forever
Defiled would be my blood, if through me,   940
And through my marriage, the maiden die!
Then in dishonor, undeserved, incredible,

---

[1] See Appendix for omitted passage: lines 920–27.

She'd suffer intolerable wrongs—
And I would be the basest of all Greeks,
No more a man than Menelaus,   945
No son of Peleus but a fiend's child,
If for his sake my name should do this butchery.

No! By Nereus, fostered by ocean's
Waves, by the father of Thetis who bore me,
By him I swear, never will Agamemnon
Lay hands upon your daughter—nor even   950
With his finger tips touch the fringe
Of her robe.[2] Calchas, the prophet, when next
He makes sacrifice will find bitter and   955
Accursed the barley and holy water.
What sort of man is a soothsayer or prophet?
I will tell you: If he is lucky
In his guessings even then he'll speak
A flock of lies and little truth, but
When his guess is wrong and unlucky,
Poof! like smoke he is nothing.
Now must I tell you, it is not on account
Of this marriage I have said these things—
No—there are many girls for marrying,   960
But I cannot endure the insult and injury
Which the lord Agamemnon has heaped upon me!

                              (*More calmly.*)

What would have been fitting, if he had wanted
This snare and pretext, then he should
Have requested from me the use of my name.
As it was, I knew nothing, and so
To your husband, chiefly through faith in me,
You surrendered your daughter.

              (*In a lower voice, after thinking the matter over.*)

Perhaps—I might have granted him use   965
Of my name—for the sake of Greece—

[2] See Appendix for omitted passage: lines 952–54.

If so the ships could sail. Nor would
I have denied help to the common cause
Of those with whom I march.

(Angry again and his voice rising.)

But now
I am nothing and nobody in the eyes
Of the army chiefs! At their convenience
They do me honor or injury. I tell you
If anyone tries to tear or separate
Your daughter from me now I will fight him.
Yes—before I go to Troy this sword
Shall know his blood in death.   970
But you, lady,
Be calm now and comforted. I make myself
Known to you as though I were a god, mighty
And strong to help. Well, I am no god, and yet—
To save the girl—I shall be godlike now!

Chorus

You have spoken, Peleus' son, words worthy   975
Of yourself and of the dread sea goddess.

Clytemnestra

How can I praise and yet not overpraise
Or stint my words to lose your graciousness?
The noble, being praised, in an odd fashion
Hate those who laud them—if too much.   980
I am ashamed to tell my piteous story;
The affliction is mine, not yours—
And yet, a good man, though he be free
From trouble, succors the unfortunate.
Have mercy—my sorrow is worthy of it.   985
For first I thought that you would be my son,
And cherished in my heart an empty dream!
But now death threatens my child, an ill omen
Perhaps for your own marriage! so

You must protect yourself as well as me!
Again and again you have said this truth   990
That if you willed, my daughter would be saved.
Do you desire that she come to clasp your knees?
It would transgress a maiden's character,
But if you wish it she shall come
And blushing lift her innocent eyes to yours.
But if I can win you without her coming,   995
In maiden pride she shall remain indoors. We
Should, as far as we may, reverence modesty.

Achilles

Oh, do not bring her here for me to see!
Let us avoid foolish scandal, for the troops
Being crowded, idle, and away from home,   1000
Love filthy gossip and foul talk.
If your daughter comes a suppliant, or never,
It is the same. This enterprise is mine—
Believe my words—to rid you of these evils.   1005
Oh may I die if I mock you in this
And only live if I shall save the girl!

Clytemnestra

Heaven bless you for helping the unfortunate.

Achilles

Listen to me and you'll succeed in this—

Clytemnestra

What do you mean? I *must* listen to you.   1010

Achilles

Then once more let us persuade her father
To a saner mood.

Clytemnestra

                        Terror of the army—
This base fear is in him.

Achilles

                    Reason can wrestle
  And overthrow terror.

Clytemnestra

                My hopes are cold on that.

                                              (Pause.)

  What must I do?

Achilles

  First this, beseech him like a suppliant   1015
  Not to kill his daughter. If he resists
  Then come to me you must. But if he yields
  To your deep wish—why then—
  I need not be a party to this affair.
  His very yielding will mean salvation.

  So, if I act by reason and not violence,
  I'll be a better friend and, too, escape   1020
  The troops' reproach. So without me you and
  Those dear to you may succeed in all.

Clytemnestra

  You've spoken wisely. What seems good to you
  I'll do. But if we fail in my great hope,   1025
  Where can I find and see you once again,
  In desperation seeking your hand and help.

Achilles

  I'll be on watch—and like a sentinel—
  But we'll appoint a place—and so avoid
  Your frantic search among the troops for me.   1030
  Do nothing to demean your heritage;
  Tyndareus' house deserves a fair report,
  Being a high name among all Greeks.

Clytemnestra

  These things shall be as you have spoken them.
  Rule me—it is my compulsion to obey.

If there are gods, you, being righteous,
Will win reward in heaven; if there are none,   1035
All our toil is without meaning.

(*Clytemnestra and Achilles go out.*)

Chorus

Oh what bridal song with Libyan flute,
With lyre dance-loving,
With reeds pipe-pealing,
Rang forth on the air,
When to Pelion came lovely haired   1040
The Graces to feast with the gods;
Gold-sandaled their feet
Stamping the ground;
On to the marriage of Peleus and Thetis,
Over the hills of the Centaurs,
Down through Pelion's woodlands,
To magnify with music's praise,   1045
The son of Aeacus.
And Phrygian Ganymede, Dardanus' child,   1050
Of Zeus favored and loved,
Into a golden bowl
Poured the libation, while
Near on the glistening sea sands, circling,   1055
The daughters of Nereus
Wove the marriage dance.

With lances of pine and a leafy crown
The reveling Centaurs and riders came   1060
To the gods' feast, and the bowls brimming
With Bacchus' gift.

Wildly they cried, "Hail Nereus' daughter,
Hail to your son, a bright light blazing
For Thessaly." So sang the prophet
Of Phoebus. And foreknowing,   1065
Chiron proclaimed his birth,
Birth of him who would come with an army

Of Myrmidons, spear-throwers,
Into Troyland for the sacking   1070
Of Priam's glorious city.
And he—they sang—will put upon his body
The armor wrought by Hephaestus,
Gift of his goddess mother,
Thetis who bore him.   1075
So the gods sang this wedding hymn
Blessing the marriage
Of Peleus, noble in birth,
And of the most favored
Of Nereus' daughters.

But you, Iphigenia, upon your head   1080
And on your lovely hair
Will the Argives wreathe a crown
For sacrifice.
You will be brought down from the hill caves
Like a heifer, red, white, unblemished,
And like a bloody victim
They will slash your throat.

You were not reared   1085
To be drawn to slaughter
By the music
Of a herdsman's pipe
But by your mother's side
Fostered to marry kings.

Oh, where now has the countenance
Of modesty or virtue   1090
Any strength,
When the blasphemer rules,
And heedless men
Thrust righteousness behind them,
When lawlessness rules law,

And no man—or his neighbor—
Fears the jealousy of God?

Clytemnestra

(*Entering and speaking to the Chorus.*)

I have come from the pavilion seeking
My husband. For he left our tent
And has been absent long. My unhappy
Child now weeps her heart out, first moaning   1100
Soft, then crying aloud, for she has heard
Of the death her father plots against her—
I speak of Agamemnon, and he comes. Now
In an instant he will be found guilty
Of this unholy crime against his child!   1105

(*Agamemnon enters.*)

Agamemnon

O daughter of Leda, I am glad
To find you now outside our tent,
For at this moment I must speak to you
Of several things not proper for a bride to hear.

Clytemnestra

What things fit so perfectly this moment?

Agamemnon

Send for the child from the pavilion   1110
To join her father. But first listen to me:
The lustral waters have now been prepared
And the barley to throw on cleansing fire;
Bridal victims are ready—their black blood
Soon to flow in honor of Artemis.

Clytemnestra

Speaking, you give all these things fair names.   1115
But for the deed of your intention—
I can find no good name for that.

(*Calling.*)

Come outside, my daughter; the will
Of your father you now know fully and well.
Come and bring your brother Orestes,
Child, and cover him with your robe.

(*Enter Iphigenia with Orestes in her arms
followed by an attendant.*)

Behold she is here, and in her coming   1120
To you now she is obedient, but as to the rest
Of this business, on her behalf and mine
I shall now speak.

Agamemnon

     Child, why are you crying?
Why do you look upon the ground and hood
Your eyes from me with your robe?

Clytemnestra

       I do not know
How I can make a beginning of my story
To you, since in equal measure the beginning,   1125
The middle, and the end is sorrow.

Agamemnon

        What has happened?
Why do you both look at me with trouble
And with terror in your eyes?

Clytemnestra

      My husband,
Answer my question with the courage of a man.

Agamemnon

Go on—I am willing. There is no need   1130
To command an answer from me.

Clytemnestra

Your child and mine—do you intend to kill her?

> (*Iphigenia, distraught, turns from her father.*
> *Attendant takes the child Orestes*
> *from her arms.*)

Agamemnon

What a horrible speech! To hold such
Accusation in the mind is vile—

Clytemnestra

Stop! Give me first an answer to this question.

Agamemnon

A reasonable question I will answer.

Clytemnestra

I ask this only—answer it.   1135

Agamemnon

> (*After a pause in which he stares at her in growing*
> *fear and agony, finally it bursts from him.*)

Oh, my fate,
August and awful! My misfortune.
Oh, what an evil demon is mine

Clytemnestra

Yours! Mine and hers! One evil fate for three
And misery for us all.

Agamemnon

> (*Turning on her suddenly.*)

Whom have I wronged?

Clytemnestra

You ask me this—your mind has lost its reason!

Agamemnon

(*To himself.*)

I am destroyed—my secret is betrayed.   1140

Clytemnestra

Listen, I know every part of this history
For I have sought it out and I know fully
Your intention. Even now your silence
Makes confession and this great groan of yours,
So with few words speak out.

Agamemnon

Then I would give you
A lie and lying would add shame   1145
To my misfortune. I will be silent.

Clytemnestra

Hear me now—
For I shall give you open speech and no
Dark saying or parable any more.
And this reproach I first hurl in your teeth,
That I married you against my will, after
You murdered Tantalus, my first husband,   1150
And dashed my living babe upon the earth,
Brutally tearing him from my breasts.
And then, the two sons of Zeus, my brothers,
On horseback came and in white armor made
War upon you. Till you got upon your knees
To my old father, Tyndareus, and he   1155
Rescued you. So you kept me for your bed.

But after that I became reconciled
To you and to your house, and you will bear
Witness that I, as your wife, have been
Blameless, modest in passion, and in honor
Seeking to increase your house so that   1160

Your coming-in had gladness and
Your going-out joy. A rare spoil for a man
Is the winning of a good wife; very
Plentiful are the worthless women.
And so I bore you this son and three daughters.
Now one of these you would tear from me.   1165
If any man should ask you why, why
Do you kill your daughter? What answer will
You make? Or must your words come from my mouth?
I kill her, you must answer, that Menelaus
May win Helen back. And so our child,
In her beauty, you pay as price for a woman
Of evil. So you buy with our best beloved   1170
A creature most loathed and hated.

But think now. If you leave me and go
To this war, and if your absence there
From me is stretched over the years,
With what heart shall I keep your halls in Argos?
With what heart look at each chair and find it
Empty of her; at her maiden chamber   1175
And it empty always; or when I sit
Down with tears of loneliness and for
A mourning that will have no end.

O child!

I shall then cry out. Who brought you to this death?
It was your father—he and no other,
And by no other's hand! This is the shame,
Agamemnon, and the retribution
You leave in your house.

Here am I

And the children you have left me. Oh, only
A little more do we need of pretext   1180
And provocation so that upon your

Homecoming we give you the welcome that
Is wholly due. No! by the gods, do not
Force me to become a woman of evil!
Or to betray you! And you, against me
Do not commit this sin! Tell me now,
After the sacrifice of your child, what prayer   1185
Can your mouth utter? What things of good
Can you ever pray for when you have
Slain the girl?

       Now you go from your home,
And if this going-out be shameful, will not
The return be evil? Tell me, in all
Conscience, how can I ask heaven to give
You any blessing? We must think the gods
Fools, if we ask blessing for the killers   1190
Of our children!

       When you return at last
To Argos, after the war, will you embrace
And kiss your daughters and your son? God forbid!
It would be sacrilege. For do you suppose
Any child of yours, when you have sent
A sister to her death, would ever look
Upon your face again, or in your eyes?

Speak to me—have you ever taken account
Of such things in any wise? Or is your thought
And need only to brandish scepters and   1195
Lead armies? Well then, here is a righteous
Offer you should have made to the army!
Achaeans, you are eager to sail for Troy—
Then cast lots to find whose daughter must die!
This would be justice—rather than slay
Your own child, a victim to the army.   1200
Or—let Menelaus—for this is his affair—

Kill *his* daughter for her mother's sake.
For look, my girl is torn from me, from me
Who have been faithful to my marriage,
But she who has sinned against her husband's bed—
She will return to prosper, and bring   1205
Her daughter home. And now at last answer me
If in anything I have failed to speak
Justly, but if my words are fair and
Truly spoken, be no longer mad, but wise.
Repent! And do not kill the girl—who is
Your child and mine.

Chorus

Agamemnon, yield to her! It is good
That you together save the child. No man
Can rightly speak against this word of mine.   1210

Iphigenia

                                        O my father—

If I had the tongue of Orpheus
So that I could charm with song the stones to
Leap and follow me, or if my words could
Quite beguile anyone I wished—I'd use
My magic now. But only with tears can I   1215
Make arguments and here I offer them.
O Father,
My body is a suppliant's, tight clinging
To your knees. Do not take away this life
Of mine before its dying time. Nor make me
Go down under the earth to see the world
Of darkness, for it is sweet to look on
The day's light.
I was first to call you father,   1220
You to call me child. And of your children
First to sit upon your knees. We kissed
Each other in our love. "O child,"

You said, "surely one day I shall see you
Happy in your husband's home. And like
A flower blooming for me and in my honor." 1225
Then as I clung to you and wove my fingers
In your beard, I answered, "Father, you,
Old and reverent then, with love I shall
Receive into my home, and so repay you
For the years of trouble and your fostering 1230
Care of me." I have in memory all these words
Of yours and mine. But you, forgetting,
Have willed it in your heart to kill me.

Oh no—by Pelops
And by Atreus, your father, and
By my mother who suffered travail
At my birth and now must suffer a second 1235
Time for me! Oh, oh—the marriage
Of Paris and Helen—Why must it touch
My life? Why must Paris be my ruin?
Father, look at me, and into my eyes;
Kiss me, so that if my words fail, 1240
And if I die, this thing of love I may
Hold in my heart and remember.

(Turning to Orestes.)

My brother, so little can you help us
Who love you, but weep with me and
Beg our father not to kill your sister.
Oh, the threat of evil is instinct,
Even in a child's heart. See, even
Without speech, he begs you, Father, 1245
Pity and have mercy on my sister's life.
Yes, both of us beseech you, this little child
And I, your daughter grown. So these words
Are all my argument. Let me win life
From you. I must. To look upon the world
Of light is for all men their greatest joy— 1250

The shadow world below is nothing.
Men are mad, I say, who pray for death;
It is better that we live ever so
Miserably than die in glory.

Chorus

O wicked Helen, through you, and through your
Marriage, this terrible ordeal has come
To the sons of Atreus and to the child.

Agamemnon

My daughter and my wife, I know what calls
To me for pity and compassion, and   1255
What does not. *I love my children!*
Did I not I would be mad indeed.
Terrible it is to me, my wife, to dare
This thing. Terrible not to dare it.

Here is my compulsion absolute:
Behold the armies, girt about by the fleet,
And with them over there, the kings of Greece   1260
With all their bronzen armor at their feet—
None of them can sail to Ilium's towers
Nor sack the famous bastion of Troy
Until, as the prophet Calchas has decreed,
I make you the victim of this sacrifice.

O child, a mighty passion seizes
The Greek soldiers and maddens them to sail
With utmost speed to that barbarian place   1265
That they may halt the plunder of marriage beds
And the rape and seizure of Greek women.
The army, angered, will come to Argos,
Slaughter my daughters, murder you and me
If the divine will of the goddess
I annul. It is not Menelaus

Making a slave of me—Nor am I here
At Menelaus' will, but Greece lays upon me   1270
This sacrifice of you beyond all will
Of mine. We are weak and of no account
Before this fated thing.

O child,

Greece turns to you, to me, and now,
As much as in us lies she must be free.[3]

[3] For omitted passage, lines 1274–75, see Appendix.

(*Agamemnon goes out. Attendant who holds Orestes
leaves the stage. Iphigenia turns
to her mother.*)

Clytemnestra

O maidens who are friendly to us—O my child,
What a terrible dying is yours.
Your father, betraying you to death,
Has fled away.

Iphigenia

Oh, pitiable am I, Mother!
The selfsame grieving song
Is ours, fallen from fate's hands.   1280
Life is no longer mine,
Nor the dayspring's splendor.
O snow-beaten Phrygian glen and Ida's
Hill: there on a day was the tender suckling thrown,   1285
Priam's child, from his mother torn,
For the doom of death; it was the herdsman
Of Ida, Paris of Ida,
So named, so named in his Trojan city.   1290
Would God they had never reared him,
Reared Alexander, herdsman of cattle,
To dwell by the silvery waters,
By the nymphs and their fountains,   1295

By that meadow green and abundant
With roses and hyacinths
Gathered for goddesses.

There on that day came Pallas   1300
And Cypris the beguiling,
Hera, and Hermes, God's messenger—
Cypris, who crushes with desire,
Pallas with her spear,   1305
And Hera, Zeus' royal wife and queen—
They came for the judging,
For the hateful battle of beauty
Which to me brings death, O maidens,
But to the Danaans glory.   1310

O my mother, my mother,
Artemis has seized me, for Ilium
A first sacrifice!
He who began my life
Has betrayed me in misery
To a lonely dying.
Oh, my wretchedness,   1315
As I see her,
Helen, doom-starred and evil;
Bitter, bitter
Is the death you bring me!
Murdered by my father—
Accursed butchery,
For I shall be slain
By his unholy hands.

Oh, if only Aulis had not taken   1320
To the bosom of her harborage
These, our ships—
With their wings of pine,
Their beaks of bronze!

Oh, if only
The breath of Zeus had not swept them
To the roadstead that faces the river.
Zeus' breath—it brings delight—
And doom—to mortals;   1325
At one time the sails laugh
In a favoring breeze,
At another, Zeus the Almighty
Blows down upon mortals
Delay and doom.
O toil-bearing race, O toil-bearing   1330
Creatures living for a day—
Fate finds for every man
His share of misery.
O Tyndareus' daughter,
What burden you have laid
Upon the Danaans   1335
Of anguish and disaster!

Chorus

    I pity you for your evil fate. Oh—
    That it had never found you out!

Iphigenia

    O Mother, there are men—I see them coming here.

Clytemnestra

    It is Achilles, son of the goddess
    For whom your father brought you here—

Iphigenia

    Maidens, open the doors, so that I may   1340
    Hide myself.

Clytemnestra

        Why do you run away, child?

Iphigenia

 I am ashamed to see him—to look
 On the face of Achilles.

Clytemnestra

       But why?

Iphigenia

 Oh, my unlucky marriage—I am ashamed—

         (Covering her face with her hands.)

Clytemnestra

 In this crisis, daughter, you can't afford
 These delicate feelings. So stay—this
 Is no time for modesty—if we can—

      *(Threatening shouts of the army are heard
         off stage. Enter Achilles.)*

Achilles

 Woman of misery and misfortune,   1345
 Leda's daughter—

Clytemnestra

    Yes, you have said what is true.
 I am she.

Achilles

        (Pauses for a moment.)

   The Argives are shouting
 A thing of terror.

Clytemnestra

    What are they shouting?

Achilles

 It is about your daughter.

Clytemnestra

     Oh, the words
 Of ill omen—you have said them now.

Achilles

    Yes, they are shouting she must be slaughtered
In sacrifice.

Clytemnestra

           And was there no one
On the other side to argue against them?

Achilles

    Yes, I spoke to the yelling crowd and so
Was in danger.

Clytemnestra

            In danger of what?

Achilles

    Of death by stoning.

Clytemnestra

             Oh—and because you
Tried to save my child?   1350

Achilles

              Yes, for that.

Clytemnestra

                        (Incredulous.)

    But who would have dared to lay a hand on you?

Achilles

                          (Bitterly.)

    Every Greek soldier.

Clytemnestra

                   (Still not believing him.)

           But your own legion
Of Myrmidons, they were there at your side?

Achilles

    And the first to threaten my death.

Clytemnestra
O my child—
Now we are lost.

Achilles
(*Bitterly.*)
They mocked me, they shouted
That I had become a slave of this marriage.

Clytemnestra
What did you say?

Achilles
I answered that they
Would never slaughter my bride.   1355

Clytemnestra
Oh, a right answer!

Achilles
My bride, whom her father had pledged to me.

Clytemnestra
Yes, and brought to you from Argos.

Achilles
They drowned my voice by their yelling
And cried me down.

Clytemnestra
Oh, the mob—what a terror
And an evil thing!

Achilles
But I will defend you!

Clytemnestra
(*Almost scornful.*)
You—one man fighting a thousand!

(Enter two armor-bearers.)

Achilles

Look!
These men are bringing me armor for that battle.

Clytemnestra

May the gods bless your courage—

Achilles

I shall be blest!

Clytemnestra

The child then shall *not* be killed?   1360

Achilles

Not if I live!

Clytemnestra

But tell me now, who will come here and try
To seize the girl?

Achilles

Men by thousands will come—
Odysseus will lead them.

Clytemnestra

Sisyphus' son?

Achilles

Yes!

Clytemnestra

Of his own will, or chosen by the army?

Achilles

He will be chosen, but glad of his appointment.

Clytemnestra

Chosen for evil, for bloodshed and murder!

Achilles

But I will keep him from the girl!   1365

Clytemnestra

(*Suddenly hysterical.*)

Will he, if she resists, drag her away?

Achilles

There is no doubt—and by her golden hair!

Clytemnestra

What *then* must I do?

Achilles

Hold fast to the child—

Clytemnestra

And so save her from murder—

Achilles

It comes to this—

Iphigenia

(*Who for some minutes has not heard them,
breaks from her revery.*)

Mother, now listen to my words. I see
Your soul in anger against your husband.
This is a foolish and an evil rage.
Oh, I know when we stand before a helpless
Doom how hard it is to bear.   1370

(*Pause.*)

But hear me now.
It is rightful and good that we thank and
Praise our friend for his eager kindness.
But you must be careful and see that he
Is not blamed by the army. Such a thing
Would win us nothing but would bring him
Utter ruin. And now hear me, Mother,
What thing has seized me and I have conceived
In my heart.

I shall die—I am resolved—   1375
And having fixed my mind I want to die

Well and gloriously, putting away
From me whatever is weak and ignoble.
Come close to me, Mother, follow my words
And tell me if I speak well. All Greece turns
Her eyes to me, to me only, great Greece
In her might—for through me is the sailing
Of the fleet, through me the sack and overthrow
Of Troy. Because of me, never more will
Barbarians wrong and ravish Greek women,   1380
Drag them from happiness and their homes
In Hellas. The penalty will be paid
Fully for the shame and seizure of Helen.
                                     And all
These things, all of them, my death will achieve
And accomplish. I, savior of Greece,
Will win honor and my name shall be blessed.
It is wrong for me to love life too deeply.   1385
I am the possessed of my country
And you, Mother, bore me for all Greece,
Not for yourself alone.

                           Wrong and injury
Our country suffers, and so thousands
Of men arm themselves, thousands more in these ships
Pick up their oars. They will dare very greatly
Against the enemy and die for Greece.
These are thousands, but I with my one life
To save, am I to prevent all? Where is   1390
The judgment of justice here? To the soldiers
Who die is there a word we can answer?
None. But consider further, is it right
For this man to make war upon all the Greeks
For one woman's sake and surely die?
Rather in war is it far better that
Many women go to their death, if this

Keep one man only facing the light
And alive.

   O Mother, if Artemis
Wishes to take the life of my body,   1395
Shall I, who am mortal, oppose
The divine will? No—that is unthinkable!
To Greece I give this body of mine.
Slay it in sacrifice and conquer Troy.
These things coming to pass, Mother, will be
A remembrance for you. They will be
My children, my marriage; through the years
My good name and my glory. It is
A right thing that Greeks rule barbarians,   1400
Not barbarians Greeks.

    It is right,
And why? They are bondsmen and slaves, and we,
Mother, are Greeks and are free.

Chorus

 Child, you play your part with nobleness.
 The fault is with the goddess and with fate.

Achilles

     O child of Agamemnon—
If I had won you as my bride, if only—   1405
I would have sworn a god had given me
Happiness. I envy Greece because you
Are hers, not mine. And you too I envy
Because Greece has chosen you, not me,
To die. Of our country with honor too
You have spoken. You gave up the fight
Against God's will and chose the thing that was
Good and was fated. And yet the more I
See of your nature—for it is noble—

Desire for our marriage overcomes 1410
My spirit.

   Listen to me, listen.
For I want to serve you and help you. Yes,
And to carry you home as my bride.
O Thetis, goddess mother, witness this
Is the truth. I am in agony to throw
Myself into battle with all the Greeks
To save you. Consider again how
Terrible a thing and how evil is death! 1415

Iphigenia

I speak this as one past hope and fear,
So listen to me. It is enough that
Helen, daughter of Tyndareus, because
Of her body hurls men into war
And to slaughter. But you, stranger and my friend,
You must not die for me or kill any man;
Only let me, if I have the strength, save Greece. 1420

Achilles

O noble heart! How can I ever add
Words of mine to these of yours, since you
Have fixed your will to die. Your soul is noble—
Who would not speak this truth! But yet—it is
Possible you will repent and alter
Your fixed mind. Then know my proposal 1425
And offer—for I come with these arms and
Shall place them by the altar directly.
I shall come, but not like the others
To suffer, but to prevent your death
And sacrifice. Oh, in a flash you can
Turn to me and prove my promises! Yes,
Even at the final second when you
See the sword thrust at your throat. For this is

A rash and hasty impulse; I will not   1430
Let you die for it. So, I shall arrive
With these arms at the goddess' altar,
And there wait and watch till you come.

(Achilles goes out, Iphigenia turns to her mother.)

Iphigenia

You make no sound, but you are weeping.
Why do you weep for me?

Clytemnestra

                 Is not this sorrow
Terrible enough to break my heart?

Iphigenia

Stop! And trust me in all of this, Mother.   1435
Do not make a coward of me.

Clytemnestra

               Daughter,
I do not want to wrong or hurt you.
Tell me what I must do.

Iphigenia

             Here is one thing I ask:
Don't shear from your head the lock of hair
Or dress yourself in mourning for my sake.

Clytemnestra

What are you saying, child? When I have lost
You forever—

Iphigenia

         No! I am not lost
But saved! And you too, through me, will be   1440
Remembered gloriously.

Clytemnestra

          Oh, what do you mean?
Is it not right that I mourn your death?

Iphigenia

No! For I say no funeral mound is
To be heaped up for me.

Clytemnestra

What? Isn't it
Ordained and rightful that there be a burying
For the dead?

Iphigenia

The altar of the goddess,
Mother, who is Zeus' daughter, will be
My grave and my monument.

Clytemnestra

O my child,
Yours are the good words and the right ones.   1445
I will obey you.

Iphigenia

That will be my memorial
As one favored by fate because I brought
Help to Greece.

Clytemnestra

Your sisters—what message
Shall I take them?

Iphigenia

O Mother, do not dress
Them in mourning.

Clytemnestra

(Nodding.)

But have you some last word
Of love that I may speak to them?

Iphigenia

(Slowly.)

Only this—
I say goodbye to them now. That is all.

(Thinking.)

Orestes—do this, nurture him and see   1450
That he comes to strength and manhood for my sake.

Clytemnestra

Embrace and look at him for the last time.

Iphigenia

(Taking him in her arms.)

Dearest—you tried to help as best you could!

Clytemnestra

(Speaking with difficulty.)

O my child, when I go home to Argos
Is there something I can do to bring you joy?

Iphigenia

(Turning her eyes slowly upon her mother.)

Yes. Do not hate *him.* Do not hate my father
Who is your husband.

Clytemnestra

Oh! Oh! Your father
Must run a course of agony and terror   1455
For your sake.

Iphigenia

Running against his will,
For the sake of Greece, he has committed me
To death.

Clytemnestra

By a treacherous plot! Unkingly
And unworthy of Atreus!

Iphigenia

(No longer listening.)

Who will lead me
To the altar, before they seize me
And drag me by my hair?

Clytemnestra

                        I—I will come with you.

Iphigenia

  No, no, that is wrong!

Clytemnestra

                    I'll go—just my hand

  On your robe—

Iphigenia

             Mother, trust me,   1460

  Here you must stay, which will be better

  For you and for me also. Let it be

  One of my father's attendants who brings me

  To the meadow of Artemis and to the place

  Where I shall be killed.

Clytemnestra

                  Oh, child,

  You are going now—

Iphigenia

                Yes.

  And not to come back again.

Clytemnestra

                      Leaving your mother—   1465

Iphigenia

  Oh, you see how hard—

Clytemnestra

               Oh, stay.

  Don't leave me, child!

                    (*She bursts into a flood of tears.*)

Iphigenia

  Stop! I forbid your crying out or any tears!

O lift up your voices,
Lift them to Artemis
In honor of my fate
And of my dying;
Shout a paean of glory
To the daughter of Zeus.
And let the host of Danaans be silent,
As the priest takes
From the basket the barley;   1470
So may the fire blaze
With the meal of purification,
And my father will turn to the right
And encircle the altar.
Then I will come
And bring to Greece
Her salvation
And a crown of victory!
Lead me on
For the sack and overthrowing   1475
Of Troy city
And the Phrygian land.
Put on my hair a wreath
Of garlands
And on my head a crown.
O drench me with the waters,
The waters of purification.
About the altar of Artemis,
About her temple,
Dance!
Let us dance in honor of Artemis,   1480
Goddess, queen and blest.
With my own blood
In sacrifice
I will wash out
The fated curse of God.
O Mother, my lady mother,   1485

Now I give you my tears
For when I come to the holy place
I must not weep.   1490
Now maidens let us join
In praise of Artemis,
Artemis in her temple
Across Chalcis strait,
Where now in Aulis gulf,
And by the narrows,
Spears are flung fiercely
In my name.   1495
O motherland Pelasgia,
Mycenae, my Mycenae
Who fostered me—

Chorus

Do you call on Perseus' citadel   1500
Wrought by the hands of the Cyclops?

Iphigenia

You fostered me
A light to Greece
I do not refuse to die for you.

Chorus

Never will your glory pass away.

Iphigenia

O dayspring   1505
Torch of God
And glorious light!
To another world I go
Out of this place
Out of time
To dwell.
And now, and now,

Beloved light
Farewell!

(Iphigenia goes out.)

Final Chorus

O look at the girl who walks   1510
To the goddess' altar
That Troy may be brought low
And the Phrygian die.
Behold, she walks
With her hair in garlands of honor,
And flung upon her body the lustral waters.
To the altar she goes
Of the goddess of bloody mind
Where she shall drip
With streams of flowing blood   1515
And die,
Her body's lovely neck
Slashed with a sword to death.
Oh, the waters await you,
The waters of purification;
Your father will pour them.
And the army too awaits you,
The mighty host of the Greeks
Awaits eagerly your death
For their sailing to Troy.   1520
But now all hail to the daughter of Zeus,
All hail to Artemis, goddess queen,
For from this maiden's death
You bring a prosperous thing!
Goddess,
You who joy in human blood,
Now be our guide and send
The armies of all the Greeks
To the land of Phrygia   1525
And to the citadel of treacherous Troy;

There give to Greece and to her spearmen
A crown of victory.
And for the king,
Agamemnon,
O touch his head
With a glory everlasting.[4]

1530

[4] See Appendix for omitted passage, lines 1532–1629.

APPENDIX

APPENDIX

Lines 920–27

Achilles

—And yet I've learned to curb   920
My vaunting spirit, when I face disaster,
Just as I don't immoderately rejoice
When triumphs come. Certainly a man schooled
Well in reason may live out his life
Calling his soul his own. At times, of course,
It's pleasant not to be overwise. Yet when
One can hold firm the will—that's profitable.   925
I was educated by the most god-fearing
Amongst all men, Chiron, and it was from him
I've learned to act in singleness of heart.

Lines 952–54

Achilles

That would reverse all values—you could then
Persuade me that Sipylus, the barbarian
Border town, is a Greek city and besides
Birthplace of all our chieftains! Or,
The opposite absurdity, that Phthia is
A name unknown to the world of men.

Lines 1274–75

Agamemnon

No longer by the barbarians in their violence
Must Greeks be robbed of their wives.   1275

Lines 1532–1629

Messenger (entering)

O daughter of Tyndareus, Clytemnestra,
Come outside the pavilion and receive
My message.

Clytemnestra (entering)

    Hearing your voice calling, I am here,
    Wretched, fearful, and in terror that you   1535
    Have come to add a new disaster
    To my present grief.

Messenger

                    It is about your child—
    I must recount a thing of awe and wonder.

Clytemnestra

    Then don't delay, but tell it as quickly
    As you can.

Messenger

    I shall, and everything, dear mistress,   1540
    You shall learn clearly from the beginning
    Unless my whirling thoughts trip up my tongue.
    When we came to Artemis' grove and to
    The flowered meadow of Zeus' daughter,
    Leading your child to the mustering ground
    Of the Achaeans, then quickly the army   1545
    Of Argives assembled.
    And when King Agamemnon saw his girl
    Walk into the grove for the sacrifice
    He groaned bitterly, and turning his head
    Wept, drawing his robe across his eyes.   1550
    But she, standing beside her father, spoke:
    "O Father, I am here at your command—
    Willingly I give my body to be   1555
    Sacrificed for my country, for all Greece.
    If it be the will of heaven, lead me
    To the goddess' altar. Prosper, I say;
    Win victory in this war and then return
    To our fatherland. But let no Argive
    Touch me with his hand. Silent, unflinching,

I offer my neck to the knife." These words   1560
She spoke, and every man hearing her wondered
At the maid's courage and nobility.
Then Talthybius, standing in the midst,
According to his office spoke, proclaiming
A holy silence to the army,
And Calchas, the prophet, unsheathing   1565
With his hand the sharp knife, laid it
In the golden basket. Then he crowned
The head of the girl. And the son of Peleus,
Taking the barley and the lustral waters,
Ran round the goddess' altar and cried out:
"O child of Zeus, O slayer of wild beasts,   1570
You who turn your disk of shining light
Through the night's shadows, receive this sacrifice
Which we make to you—we the Achaean host
And the king Agamemnon—unblemished blood
From the neck of a fair girl. And grant
That ungrieved now the fleet may sail;   1575
And grant this too that we and our spears spoil
The battlements of Troy." Then Atreus' sons
And the whole army stood with eyes bent on
The earth. And the priest, taking the knife,
Uttered his prayer, and scanned her neck to strike
His blow. Oh, then I stood with my head
Bowed, and a great anguish smote my heart—   1580
But suddenly a miracle came to pass.
Clearly all heard the blow strike home—
But after, with no man knowing where or how,
The maiden vanished from the earth.
Then the priest with a great voice cried aloud
And the whole army echoed him—this when
They saw the portent which a god had sent   1585
But no man had foreknown. Though our eyes saw,
It was a sight incredible, for a
Panting hind lay there on the earth, great

To behold and fair indeed; the goddess'
Altar freely ran with the creature's blood.
At this Calchas spoke and with joy you must   1590
Believe: "O commanders of the allied
Armies, behold this victim which the goddess
Has laid upon the altar, a mountain hind
Rather than the maid; this victim she receives
With joy. By this no noble blood   1595
Stains her altar. Gladly she accepts
This offering and grants a fair voyage
For the attack on Troy. Let every sailor
Then be glad, and go to the galleys,
For on this day we must leave the hollow   1600
Bays of Aulis, and cross the Aegean sea."
Then when the victim had been burned
Wholly to cinder in Hephaestus' flame,
He prayed for the army's safe return.
After all this King Agamemnon sent me
To report to you and tell what fortune   1605
Had come from heaven and what deathless glory
He had won for Greece. And I who saw
This thing, being present, report it now to you.
Clearly your child was swept away to heaven;
So give over grief and cease from anger
Against your husband. No mortal can foreknow   1610
The ways of heaven. Those whom the gods love
They rescue. For think, this day beheld
Your child die, and come alive again.

Chorus

With what gladness I hear the messenger's
Report! Your child he tells us is alive
And with the gods in heaven.

Clytemnestra

O child! what god has stolen you from me?   1615
How can I ever call to you? How know

That this is not a story merely told
That I may have relief from bitter pain?

Chorus

Behold King Agamemnon comes to us,
And the same story he will tell to you.   1620

                                        (*Enter Agamemnon.*)

Agamemnon

My lady, may we now be happy
In our daughter's destiny. Truly she
Dwells now in fellowship with the gods.
Now must you take this little son of ours
And journey home. The army's eyes are on
The fleet. It will be long, long,
Before my greeting comes to you again   1625
On the return from Troy. Meantime
May all go well with you!

Chorus

With joy, son of Atreus, sail on
To the Phrygian land,
With joy return,
Bringing glorious spoil from Troy!